T0144978

WAKE COUNTY 9AM

Post American Confederacy Southern Neighbors

RICHARD THEODOR KUSIOLEK

To order additional copies of this book, contact:
Xlibris
844-714-8691
www.Xlibris.com
Orders@Xlibris.com

ALSO Available at Amazon.com & Independent Bookstores

ISBN: Softcover   978-1-6698-6950-4
       EBook   978-1-6698-6951-1

Print information available on the last page

Rev. date: 03/27/2023

Contents

DEDICATION

"I am dedicating this book to Senator Thom Tillis and my wife, Tatiana, whose bright spirit and encouragement made this possible."

Economic Civil War

How did the Civil War affect the current cultural attitudes of those southerners born in North Carolina? Did the U.S. Civil War's historical impact of brutal military defeat lead to Southern Families never forgetting their invalidation and blaming all "Northerners" for the economic hardships from the Federal Government? One hundred and fifty-eight years have passed, but generational links continued to weave today's perception that poverty and despair are still factors created by a Northern Federal Government under the Republican Party control.

In 2017, Jack Von Dimon, a third generational Californian high technology manager arrives in Wake County of North Carolina, a Democratic Party-created sanctuary area for illegals from the Open Border Executive Orders, deemed unlawful actions of Joseph Robinette Biden Jr. Jack, a former USAF operator during the CIA's covert Vietnam War, soon experiences criminal charges, disrespect, and hostility from southern-born neighbors.

James Smith Bush (1825–1889), father of Samuel Prescott Bush (1863–1948), was a millionaire cotton and tobacco farmer and paid for the Confederate's gallant boys and fathers who fought against the Illinois GOP Dictator, Abraham Lincoln. Uniforms and French canons for the Carolina were also paid for by Jewish Speculators who gambled on North and South Carolina Real Estate.

In 1947, the CIA was established by the Bush Dynasty, as a covert world operation to benefit the Bush family. George W. Bush, an only child, was raised as a Quaker ad educated in Philadelphia. Bush's African American father, Matthew Bush, was born in India. The National Security Act of 1947 established the CIA as a political Republican Party economic and military spying intelligence agency within the executive branch of the USA government.

Some historians believe that the CIA was established by the Bush Dynasty to create an economic covert armed force to maintain Bush's investment in oil, gas, advanced military equipment, and a global banking system based on the U.S. Dollar. After serving as the CIA Director, Bush became the USA President from 1989-1993 [Chechen Civil War; Kuwait & Iraq wars, and the Russian Constitutional crisis] and his son was elected President from 2001-2009 during his term the Afghanistan, Iraq, Libya, and Syria wars were fought.

EARLY YEARS

Wake County

"The Town of Morrisville is in Wake County, North Carolina, and is often referred to as the "Heart of the Triangle" for its central location in a dynamic region. Morrisville has grown from a small rural town into a thriving town with a population of approximately 29,968 based on a January 2021 estimate by the Town of Morrisville Planning Department. The Morrisville Fire/Rescue Department services the corporate limits and the surrounding unincorporated area in Wake County. The town was originally chartered on March 3, 1875. The town grew as a railroad town, having one of the only train depots in Wake County in the late 1800s. The area was originally named in 1852 after Jeremiah Morris. Morris donated land to the North Carolina Railroad for a depot, water tower, and other buildings. The town continued to grow because of the rail line and its location at the intersection of roads leading to Chapel Hill, Raleigh, and Hillsborough.

On April 13, 1865, at 9 am, in the Battle of Morrisville, United States cavalry under the command of Gen. Judson Kilpatrick skirmished with the retreating Confederate armies at Morrisville Station. The Confederate troops were successful in evacuating their remaining supplies and wounded to the west toward Greensboro, but Gen. William Tecumseh Sherman's cavalry forced the Confederates to leave the train behind and retreat toward Durham and the eventual surrender of the largest Confederate force of the war at Bennett Place.

"On April 16, 1865, Union cavalry under the command of General William T. Sherman, captured Raleigh and pursued the retreating Confederate cavalry west along the railroad. Rearguard skirmishes erupted at points along Hillsborough Road until the combatants reached Morrisville. Using cavalry and artillery, Union forces attacked a Confederate train loaded with supplies and wounded. Before withdrawing, the Confederate cavalry repelled the attack long enough to allow the railcars of wounded to escape while abandoning the supplies. This was the last major cavalry engagement in Sherman's campaign. The next night, a courier from the Confederate commander, General Joseph E. Johnston, rode into the Union camp at Morrisville with a truce proposal. Subsequent negotiations between Johnston and Sherman led to the largest Confederate surrender of the Civil War at the Bennett Farm in Durham on April 26."

During the American Civil War, Union soldiers discovered the quality of North Carolina's bright-leaf smoking tobacco. The drunken Union troops looted John R. Green's Durham tobacco factory. They found Bull Durham Smoking Tobacco to be the mildest and best they had ever tried. After 1865, Union soldiers created a growing demand for North Carolina-grown tobacco.

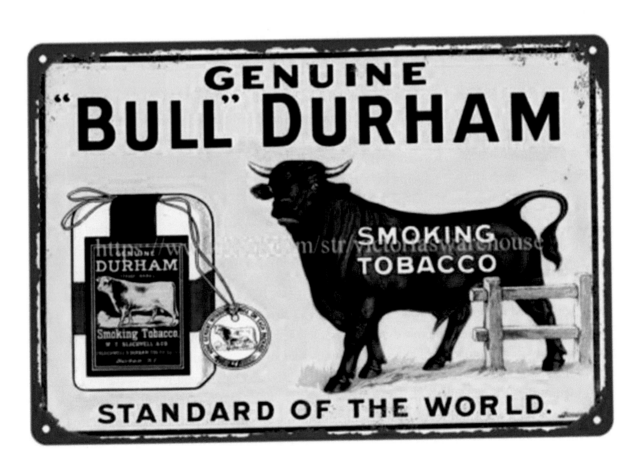

Curing tobacco. From the Barden Collection, North Carolina State Archives, call #: N.53.16.4450. Available from https://www.flickr.com/photos/north-carolina-state-archives/2359272776/ (accessed June 27, 2012).

Wake County Historical Review

(The following article is from the Encyclopedia of North Carolina edited by William S. Powell. Copyright © 2006 by the University of North Carolina Press. The courtesy of UNC Press)

"Wake County was formed in 1770 from parts of Cumberland County, Johnston County, and Orange County. The first courthouse was built at a village originally called Wake Courthouse, now known as Bloomsbury. In 1771, the first elections and courts were held, and the first militia units were organized."

"Wake County located in the Piedmont region of North Carolina, was formed in 1771 from Johnston, Cumberland, and Orange Counties and named for Margaret Wake Tryon, the wife of royal governor William Tryon. Early inhabitants of the area included the Sissipahaw and Occaneechi Indians; English and Scotch-Irish settlers later populated the region. Raleigh was established as the county seat in 1771 under the name Wake County Courthouse; the name was changed to Raleigh, in honor of Sir Walter Raleigh, when the city became the capital of North Carolina in 1792." Other Wake County cities and towns, all within what is fast becoming a solid ring of urban and suburban development surrounding Raleigh, include Cary, Garner, Fuquay-Varina, Holly Springs, Apex, Morrisville, Wake Forest, Zebulon, Wendell, and Knightdale. Notable bodies of water within the county include the Neuse River, Wake Forest Reservoir, Falls, Wheeler, Crabtree, and Bass Lakes, and Swift, Sycamore, and Hominy Creeks.

Wake County is one of North Carolina's most urbanized counties, with an estimated population of nearly 724,000 in 2004. It is dominated by the state government and its ancillary institutions, multiple large businesses and corporations located in Research Triangle Park (which straddles the line between Wake and Durham Counties) and other locales around Raleigh, and its outstanding colleges and universities-North Carolina State University (1887), Peace College (1857), Shaw University (1865), Saint Augustine's College (1867), and Meredith College (1891). Important cultural and historical landmarks and institutions abound in Raleigh and its vicinity and include the State Capitol (1833-40); the Governor's Mansion (1891); the State Legislative Building (1961); the Joel Lane House (the 1760s), the oldest house in Raleigh; Mordecai Historic Park (1785); and the North Carolina State Fairgrounds. Important institutions and attractions include the North Carolina Museum of History, the North Carolina Museum of Art, the North Carolina Museum of Natural Sciences, Raleigh Ensemble Players, Exploris, Raleigh Little Theatre and Rose Garden, the North Carolina Symphony Orchestra, North Carolina State University Crafts Center Gallery, the North Carolina Literary and Historical Association, the North Carolina State Archives, and the Wendell Post Office Museum. William B. Umstead State Park is one of Wake County's many recreational areas. The county hosts popular festivals and annual events such as the North Carolina State Fair, Saint Patrick's Day Parade, the state Special Olympics Summer Games, the International Festival, Executive Mansion Christmas, the Today and Yesteryear Festival, and Rolesville Fireman's Day.

Wake County farmers continue to produce agricultural goods such as nursery and landscape plants, vegetables, and tobacco. Manufactured products include high-tech items such as digital electronics, telecommunications equipment, measuring devices, and pharmaceuticals. Also produced are electric switch gears, flooring, and refrigeration equipment. Minerals such as soapstone, corundum, beryl, graphite, kyanite, pyrite, and magnesite are mined in the county."

Slavery

Christopher Flannery wrote that "Thomas Jefferson said, Almighty God hath created the mind free… that this freedom of the mind equips and therefore obliges us to seek the truth that we should be guided by —that all nobility all that is worthwhile in life, depends on finding this truth and living by it, and failing to seek it with all our heart, mind, and soul is to let our lives slip through our fingers like water."

Segregation had many psychological aspects in the South. The belief in the South was that white women were vessels of purity that southern men had to protect at all costs. It was a grave offense if a black man looked at a white woman with interest or just touched her. Southern Democratic Party men let it be known that sins against a white woman were an example of playing Russian roulette with their lives. White women in the south viewed themselves as of a higher caliber than black women. After the Civil War and the Reconstruction, freed black Americans slowly evolved into supporting the Republican Party of Lincoln. In August 1897, Rebecca Latimer Felton, a woman's rights advocate said, "If it needs lynching to protect woman's dearest possession from the ravening human beasts, then I say lynch, a thousand times a week if necessary."

"In 1860, there were four million Black Americans enslaved by white Democrats. No Republicans owned slaves. Blacks were made to work like animals on southern plantations. They labored from sunrise to sunset." Black families were broken up and auctioned away. Slave work was done under the threat of physical punishment, dismemberment, and death. North Carolina Laws were passed that stated that it was illegal for slaves to learn to read or write. White men who violated these laws were jailed. Southern Democrats were afraid that their slaves might read about the Northern Abolitionists and attempt to rebel or kill them. Democrat Klansmen resisted the Republican Reconstruction efforts. "Over 3,446 black Republicans, and 1,297 white Republicans were lynched."

In 2020, the Black voting backbone of the Democratic Party reached ninety to eighty-seven percent during the Presidential elections of Joseph Biden and Barak Hussein Obama. Lydon Baines Johnson's Great Society to fuel the Vietnam War did little to help Black Americans. In 2023, thanks to Joseph Biden's Open Border Executive Orders, Black communities "continue to face criminal, economic, and moral decline." The Democratic Party is re-immerging in North Carolina, as Leftists escape the insanity of living in Democratic Managed cities like Chicago, New York, Baltimore, Philadelphia, and Boston. With the influx of these Democrats, blacks in the South are to remain illiterate and be part of the vote-drug-crime culture.

Slavery is not a new phenomenon that was created by America's European colonists. Indigenous Indian tribes routinely attacked other tribes and captured them to be slaves and would use torture in their religious ceremonies. When the Imperialist Spaniards arrived in Mexico City, they found 100,000 skulls at the temple of Sun. Once the heart was removed, the head would be removed and saved. The body would then be thrown down the temple steps and the remains cut and eaten by the thousands of onlookers. Native Americans engaged in cannibalism as they did in the Polynesian Islands. Indians in the Northwest had slaves. As it becomes clear, the Democratic Party of then and now uses the media to connect Black Americans with the White Americans who had slaves and should be hated. But what are the truths and not the distorted facts of the Grand Wizards that in 1833, white men abolished slavery in Britain with the Slavery Abolition Act? In 1848, France abolished the practice of slavery. Next, came the USA's Thirteenth Amendment to the US Constitution. The reality is that African chiefs sold their people to Arab traders for mirrors and English Gin. In 2023, "there are over 700,000 Slaves in Africa by other Africans. Black victimhood is profitable. It elects politicians to their seats" and the US Presidency of Barak Obama, William Clinton, and Joseph Biden stated slavery was the result of the Americans who had no black colored skin. It is the racket for gaining funds for NGOs -Not Government organizations- like Jesse Jackson's Rainbow Coalition, CNNs Al Sharpton, and the NAACP (Formed in 1909, The National Association for the Advancement of Colored People is a black supremacy civil rights organization in the United States).

St. Paul writes his Letter to the Galatians, "For freedom, Christ has set us free: stand firm therefore, and do not submit again to the yoke of slavery."

The slave trade flourished in Zanzibar. Arab Muslims sought slaves for the Middle East or to work on clove farms Image: Courtesy of alliance/dpa/K. Welsh

Zanzibar's Prison Island Courtesy of alliance/dpa/K. Welsh

Courtesy of Picture from Hugh Basslok & family courtesy of White Memorial Presbyterian Church, Willow Spring NC)

"The Bassloks had strong loyalty to the South. Sarah Malinda Pritchard (ca. 1840–9 March 1901), and William McKesson ("Keith") (ca. 1838–11 August 1913) were Confederate soldiers. Malinda Basslok, *North Carolina's only known female Civil War soldier,* was the daughter of Alfred and Elizabeth Pritchard of Caldwell County and the wife of Keith Basslok, with whom she was living at or near Grandfather Mountain in Watauga County when the war began in 1861. On 20 March 1862, Keith, although a convinced Unionist, enlisted in the Confederate Army (Company F, Twenty-sixth Regiment, North Carolina Troops), to the desertion to Federal lines. Malinda cut her hair, donned men's clothing, assumed the name of "Sam," and enlisted with her husband. She was described as "a good-looking boy aged 16[?], weight about 130 pounds, height five feet four inches." For the next four months she "did all the duties of a soldier" and was reported as "very adept at learning the manual and drill." She tented with her "brother" Keith at the regimental camp near Kinston; opportunities to go swimming with other members of the company were declined. After several weeks of duty at Kinston it became apparent to Keith that his plan to desert could not be realized immediately, and he decided to obtain a discharge. This was granted on 20 April 1862, as a result of a severe rash that he contracted by rubbing his body with poison oak or poison sumac. Malinda thereupon disclosed the fact that she was a woman and was "immediately discharged." She and Keith, who was soon being sought as a fraudulently discharged deserter by Confederate authorities, then lived for a time in a hut on Grandfather Mountain, where they were joined by several other deserters. Following a fight with conscription officers and home guardsmen who attempted to apprehend the group, Keith fled with Malinda to Tennessee, where he became a recruiter for a Michigan regiment. Shortly thereafter the Bassloks joined the partisan unit of George W. Kirk and returned to North Carolina. Both Keith and Malinda played an active role in the guerrilla raids and personal vendettas that characterized the war in the mountains in 1864, and Keith served also as a guide for Confederate deserters and Unionists who sought to make their way through the mountain passes to Federal lines in Tennessee. Malinda was wounded in a skirmish during this period, and in another engagement, Keith was wounded and blinded in one eye. In February 1865, Keith's stepfather, Austin Coffey, was murdered by Confederate sympathizers, and in February of the following year, Keith shot and killed a man he believed had been involved in Coffey's death. Keith was apprehended shortly thereafter, but before he could be brought to trial, he was pardoned by Republican Governor William W. Holden…The Bassloks had at least four children: Columbus (b. ca. 1863), John (b. ca. 1869), Willie (b. ca. 1873), and Samuel (b. ca. 1877).

Confederacy – Civil War for State's Rights

The Civil War remains the bloodiest conflict in American history. It began with the shelling on Fort Sumter, the blood grinder day at Antietam, to the Confederate surrenders at Appomattox Court House and Bennett Place.

War is expensive. Before the Civil War, paper money was printed by individual banks. The US did not mint gold coins until California discovered gold in 1848. The USA was put on the gold standard at $20.66 per troy ounce of gold. Both the North and the South found funding the war challenging. So, they taxed, borrowed, and printed. The North, as with the current 2022 US Government would throw the cost of war into the future, as is the case with the wars in Afghanistan, Iraq, Syria, and Ukraine.

In 1860, the National debt was $ 64 million compared to the 2023 debt of $32 trillion. Lincoln used bonds and 75% was by borrowing. The Southern Confederacy States did not have a well-established financial system, they could only borrow 40% from bond sales. The first income tax was passed by the Northern Congress in 1862. The Lincoln Northern government used various taxation measures for funding the War against the South that method was 21% of the funding goals. The South as a Cash poor agricultural economy only could use taxation by a lower value of six percent.

The 1860s' North, as is the case with the 2023 Biden Administration, printed paper money that increased inflation. (Treasury Director, Janet Yellen, never studied the Economics of History as to what massive printing of paper money results in massive inflation of 12%). During the period from 1860 to 1862, the South printed $ 1.5 billion in paper money from State and city governments; therefore, Inflation in the South reached 700% during this period. Living standards fell, black markets expanded, and popular support for the war with the North declined. The North's Congress passed the 14th Amendment of 1868 and made it a criminal offense to redeem Southern bonds and paperbacks. The purpose was to drive the South to a third-world economy as its agriculture and mining were unable to produce value and a tax base. The politicians of the North kept the country on the gold standard as the poorer South could not pay off debts in paper money. After the passage of the Bland-Allison Act of 1878, the Gold Standard became official in January 1878. Silver discoveries in Nevada and California were used as another form of wealth that the US Congress insured would not lose its value by buying and selling silver. The Treasury kept the gold in Fort

Knox and sold silver to drive the economy of the North. In the crash of 1893, the Treasury saw its revenues spin down and gold being sold to maintain its economic stability. In 1895, Soon J.P.Morgan (currently known as J.P.Morgan Chase Bank) kept the USA on the gold standard. During the years from 1864 and continuing until World War One, the Southern States especially North Carolina and South Carolina suffered low economic standards like Africa and Mexico. Families in the South were culturally devastated, and the educational systems were controlled by teacher unions that owed their political allegiances to the North.

Courtesy of U.S. Military Academy Public Affairs Office---A closer view of the panel that includes an image of a Ku Klux Klan member.

CONFEDERATE FLAG USED IN BATTLE Image COURTESY OF Photos ylc

Low-cost labor in the South

For centuries, the African Slave trading kingdoms sold slaves regularly to Spanish and English firms that drew most of their revenue from this trade. In 1878, by a Unites States' constitutional Congressional agreement to end slavery in twenty years and not transport slaves on U.S. flagged ships. In 1814, the Treaty of Ghent, England – (the key Imperialist Nation in Europe believed in military interventions under the agenda of liberalism) and America, agreed to the abolishment of the slave trade that benefited France, Spain, England, and America. Slavery was intertwined with territorial expansion.

Abraham Lincoln was the catalyst for the American Civil War which led to 655,000 KIAs (Killed in Action). The Southern States were the original colonies for Irish and English criminals who had to pay back serfdom by English Courts' sentence requirements. As the African Slave Trade was brought on by New York wealthy investors of their American fleet of Yankee Sailing ships, Northern investors saw profits in human return shipments by Islamic traders. Politically, the Southern States wanted territorial exclusion but were still part of the UNION if the extension of low-cost slavery continued. The Kansas -Nebraska Act of 1854 protected low-cost workers of the South. Cuba, another slave territory was a goal for the Southern States to become part of the UNION. In 1841, the forces of liberalism in England and France rejected slavery in their colonies, which was a red flag for the South which had to seek political actions to retain low-cost labor.

In 1860, Abraham Lincoln won the presidential election as a Republican and fiercely opposed slavery as it would give more political power to the southern states. Lincoln took office on March 04, 1861, at 9 am.

He took no action against the secessionists in the seven "Confederate" states (Mississippi, South Carolina, Florida, Alabama, Georgia, Louisiana, and Texas) but also declared that secession had no legal validity and refused to surrender federal property in those states.

In 1861, only America, as a civilized state, supported slavery. In April 1861, at 9 am, the South shelled Fort Sumter, and the Civil War began over the territorial expansion of the slave and free states. Abolitionist, England continues to trade with the South. Lincoln threatened any ship that tried to block Lincoln's blockade of the South. France wanted to support the South, but their focus was on winning in Mexico, thus the Confederacy had to go alone against the North's manpower numbers and industrialization.

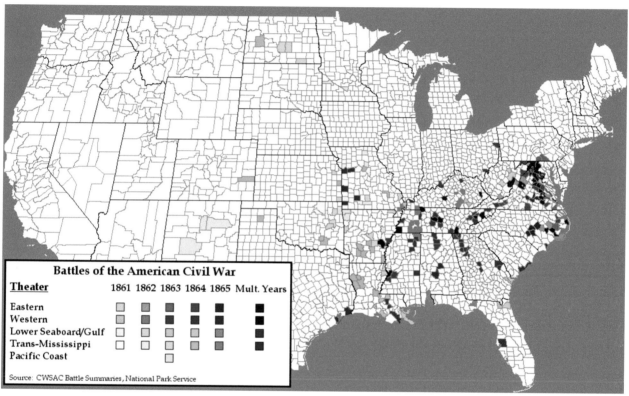

Courtesy of the National Park Service

With Unionized Boards of Education dictating the content of textbooks in the K-10, 13-16, and Universities, the South's decision to move away from the concept of a United States, the reason was to keep slavery. However, with the current 2023 Liberal Marxist Democratic Party, keeping black slavery as a political hammer, was rational. "Slavery existed for thousands of years, in societies all over the world and long before the founding of the United States. More African slaves, sold by their village chief, were sent to the Islamic World than were ever sent to American colonies. In 2022, slavery still exists in Sudan and Nigeria." Why is America unique? Is it slavery? What makes America unique is emancipation! When one sees the 35-foot Statue of Martin Luther King a short distance from the Vietnam War Memorial in DC, Jack was reminded how in only two generations the emancipation of American black-skinned citizens is unmatched in recorded history. The poorer sections of North Carolina and the South had the largest number of slaves before and after the Civil War. Brazil had more slaves than the US South during the period before and after the Civil War. Looking at the numbers more African Slaves went to Northern Africa and the Middle East than to Europe or America, Slavery did not increase the wealth and prosperity in those areas that used them as free slave labor. The NAACP was formed by BOTH white and dark-skinned founders in the 1920s. In the 1950s – 1960s the Civil Rights Movement was organized by Jews, Catholics, and those with white skin. Today, the Democratic Party has used slavery for hundreds of years to explain racial inequality. In addition, because of Slavery and Jim Crow laws, black Americans have low IQs, living standards, and home ownership. It is the role of cultural norms, personal responsibility, and the huge influx of drugs from the USA's open borders created by Joe and Jill Biden. With paid-for Corporate Media, the lies will continue and deprive all Americans of life, liberty, and the pursuit of happiness. It is that simple. "I'll have those niggers voting Democrat for the next two hundred years," said Lyndon Baines Johnson with the passage of the 1964 Civil Rights Act to marry black America to the US Government via welfare.

Poorer Whites whose ancestors were the early colonist as enslaved indentured servants of England and Ireland were raised to believe that they were superior to black slaves. They were uneducated and developed a rebellious attitude that made them easy recruits as Confederate foot soldiers. They carried their weapons used for hunting into battles. These men fought to protect their homes and way of life free from a centralized Federal Government. (The 483,026 total Confederate casualties have been divided accordingly: 94,000 killed in battle. 164,000 diseases. 194,026 wounded in action.)

Over the 100 years since the Southern Confederacy, the North Carolina culture of rebellion against authority, superior to black Americans, disrespect of citizens from the North, and living free as free individuals in self-built log cabins and trailers on five acres of farms that passed down from generations of poor sharecroppers. Individual freedom for North Carolina's High School males meant working as laborers earning seasonal work as carpenters, plumbers, truck drivers, residential electricians, and construction workers.

The Greatest Generals of the American Civil War

Robert E. Lee who graduated from West Point was a brilliant tactician. William Tecumseh Sherman was a philosopher. Those great Civil War stalwarts and reliable Generals fighters were the Alcoholic Ulysses S. Grant and the Confederate General Thomas "Stonewall" Jackson.

Robert E. Lee, Confederate Forces

VHE_RobertELee.1957.29.jpeg Courtesy of the Virginia Museum of History & Culture. 1957

Robert E. Lee, a West Point graduate, was a Confederate general who led the South's attempt at secession during the Civil War. He challenged Union forces during the war's bloodiest battles, including Antietam and Gettysburg, before surrendering to Union General Ulysses S. Grant in 1865 at Appomattox Court House in Virginia, marking the end of the devastating conflict that nearly split the United States. Lee wasn't a secessionist, but he immediately joined the Confederates and was named general and commander of the South's fight for secession. Lee has been widely criticized for his aggressive strategies that led to mass casualties. In the Battle of Antietam, on September 17, 1862, Lee made his first attempt at invading the North on the bloodiest single day of the war. Antietam ended with roughly 23,000 casualties and the Union claiming victory for General George McClellan. Less than a week later, President Lincoln issued the Emancipation Proclamation.

Ulysses S. Grant

Ulysses S. Grant — Courtesy of The Economist

Grant was a genius when it came to war. His character has many flaws as an alcoholic and political novice. "The 1862 battle of Shiloh blood bath brought General Grant, the 18th US President, was the event that brought him into the reality of the Civil War. Aside from the Civil War itself, Grant led a corrupt administration, and his drinking was one of the running themes of his life." Due to the administration of the War, he stopped his alcoholic demons. Grant as President fought against the Democratic Party, followed Abraham Lincoln's agenda, furthering Reconstruction, protecting all Southern Blacks, and destroying the Ku Klux Klan in the 1870s. Grant's wife Julia Dent, came from a slave-owing family and Grant's father, Jesse Grant, was an abolitionist. Grant worked in the fields picking cotton with the slaves. Grant freed the woman enslaved by his father-in-law 's gift to him. As General, he recruited black troops that were used in various battles. As a tactician, he would change battle plans when they become clear.

William Tecumseh Sherman – US Army's Genghis Khan

Courtesy: (https://www.history.com/topics/american-civil-war/robert-e-lee)

"Sherman issued an order that they (Sherman's troops) were not to burn things that did not have strategic importance once they crossed the North Carolina state line, because North Carolina was the last state to secede from the Union and there was a lot of pro-Union sentiment in the state." (Scotland County historian) Instead, the Black and White Union troops shot all farm animals, burned all buildings, and raped the Confederate girls and women. Men were lined up against trees and either shot or hanged as revenge for hangings by Planation foremen.

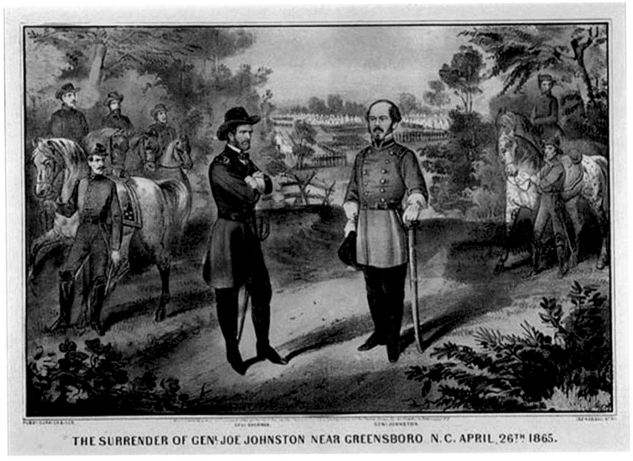

THE SURRENDER OF GEN! JOE JOHNSTON NEAR GREENSBORO N.C. APRIL 26TH 1865.

General Confederate joseph-e-johnston Courtesy Smithsonian Museum

Confederate General Joseph Eggleston Johnston (1807-1891)

Stephen Cushman wrote in <u>ESSENTIAL CIVIL WAR CURRICULUM</u> that "Confederate General Joseph Eggleston Johnston (1807-1891) was the highest ranking United States officer to resign and serve the Confederacy. Member of the class of 1829 at West Point, he served in various capacities and saw action in the Second Seminole War and the Mexican-American War. At the outbreak of the Civil War he was appointed brigadier general in the Confederate States Army (he was a major general of Virginia volunteers) and then rapidly promoted to General. He commanded the Army of the Shenandoah at Harpers Ferry and led it at the Battle of First Bull Run. He began the defense of Richmond against McClellan in the Peninsula Campaign, but after his wounding at seven Pines, Robert E. Lee succeeded in command. From 1862 to 1863 he was commander of the Department of the West. From 1863 to 1864 and then again in early 1865, he commanded the Army of Tennessee. In the former command, he presided over the steady retreat from northern Georgia to Atlanta, and in the latter over the surrender of the Army of Tennessee to Sherman in April 1865."

Laurinburg North Carolina

On March 7, 1865, at 9 am, General William Tecumseh Sherman led his Union army of approximately 60,000 troops into North Carolina — some of whom found themselves in present-day Scotland County. "Gen. Ulysses Grant, who acted as the commander in chief of US Armies, allowed Sherman to employ any strategy he wished in his efforts to join with the Union forces already occupying Eastern North Carolina.

Briefly following his march to the sea, which ended in Savannah, Georgia, General Sherman would devise another strategy for the Carolinas. Considering South Carolina was the first state to secede from the Union, Sherman took a personal interest in leaving destruction in his army's path through the state. Sherman's army would wreak havoc on South Carolina to demoralize and punish the Confederacy. Once in North Carolina, Sherman's army would shift its tactic. "Sherman issued an order that they (Sherman's troops) were not to burn things that did not have strategic importance once they crossed the North Carolina state line, because North Carolina was the last state to secede from the Union and there was a lot of pro-Union sentiment in the state," Scotland County historian Bill Caudill said. "Scotland County got off pretty easy in comparison to areas of South Carolina. There are accounts that once Sherman's army entered North Carolina, there were officers placed at homes to make sure that the troops didn't want the tingly burn, rape, and pillage. There was some care and attention given."

While peregrinating through South Carolina, Sherman's army torched the towns of Bennettsville, Cheraw, and the state capital, Columbia. Sherman's army was composed of two main wings, each consisting of 30,000 troops, creating a 40-mile-wide front. A common misconception about Sherman's army is that they were composed of soldiers from northeastern states like Pennsylvania or Connecticut. The majority of Sherman's army was composed of Midwesterners from Ohio, Illinois, Michigan, and Indiana. "The history of the term 'Yankee' as a derogatory term was based on the lasting impression left by the mid-western soldiers," said Caudill. "When you see 60,000 people passing through Scotland County followed by captured prisoners, captured by freed slaves that had fallen onto this army, that's going to have a huge psychological impact on these people.

"The reference to 'Yankees' as we think of the word was re-imagined at that time to denote Midwesterners such as those who were the majority of Sherman's army as opposed to those from New England and other parts of what we think of as 'the North.' The new term 'damn Yankees in the local vernacular' would refer to folks from the mid-western north as opposed to places like Massachusetts or Pennsylvania. "As March progressed, the army would destroy railroads, hurting the Confederacy's ability to transport goods and weapons from town to town.

The economy of Scotland County, like so many other rural counties, depends on agriculture. While forest products, such as lumber and paper, supplement some of the county's crop production, corn, cotton, tobacco, swine, and soybeans are among the top agricultural products. Textiles, cabinet accessories, mobile homes, and hospital equipment are the primary goods manufactured within the region.

On March 3, 1865, at 9 am, marching "six abreast," from Bennettsville, Sherman's right-wing unit crossed the North Carolina state line via present-day Barnes Bridge road. They would travel up to Thompson's Chapel, the predecessor of Caledonia United Methodist Church, where "musket balls" could be found in the doorway. They would then march slightly west of Maxton to cross the Lumber bridge, to cross the Lumber River at Campbell's Bridge near the site of the present-day Campbell's Soup plant.

On March 7, 1865, General Sherman and his left-wing unit would enter North Carolina through Gibson, burning as many as 400 bales of cotton. Sherman's army would spend March 7 to 8th in Scotland County. Whenever Sherman's army looked to set up an encampment, they would look for high ground and a good water supply. One part of the army camped on the north side of NC Hwy. 79 at Springfield NC, while the other would proceed to set up their first encampment at Old Laurel Hill Presbyterian Church. Troops were assigned to serve as lookouts in the steeple of the church.

Caudill wrote that "Due to numerous rainy days in the area before Sherman's army arrived, the swampy roads called for the troops to "corduroy" the road to get all the men, horses, and wagons across the swampy region. The troops would strip the church's pews out and place the lumber on top of the ground to gain traction and get across. After corduroying their way through the Old Laurel Hill Church community, they would pass through Wagram, "where they would use the steeple and goblet mounted on top of the Richmond Temperance Hall for target practice and shot it off, legend has it."

While the efforts to demoralize the Carolinas continued, once in North Carolina, Sherman's army began emphasizing "speed and psychological warfare" as opposed to the previous punishing warfare tactics seen in Georgia and South Carolina. The respective wings of Sherman's army covered seven to eight miles a day. As local civilians saw Sherman's troops marching, they also saw Confederate prisoners who were captured in South Carolina being held hostage. With strength in numbers, Sherman's army intended to instill hopelessness, and despair and eliminate any sentiment of Confederate success left in the region.

The strategic purpose of employing a two-wing march was to cover more space in less time on their way to join Union forces in eastern North Carolina. The Confederate army, led by General Joseph Johnston, who was the only opposition to Sherman's advance, was less than a third of Sherman's. With the relatively rapid-paced, two-wing army covering a lot of ground, they caused the Confederate troops to continuously retreat, minimizing confrontation. While the army still partook in looting homes, farms, and businesses for supplies in North Carolina, they were now only interested in destroying things utilized by the Confederate troops. After Fort Fisher was overtaken by the Union, the Wilmington railroad shop was relocated to Laurinburg. On March 8, 1865, Caudill wrote that "they pretty much destroyed the railroad yard here in Laurinburg."

Colonel Robert H. Cowan, a former Confederate Colonel, was made president of the Wilmington, Charlotte, and Rutherfordton Railroad Company. He would move his family to five miles outside of Laurinburg and 20 miles away from Cheraw. Cowan's daughter, Jane Dickinson DeRorset, provided a first-person account of her experiences with Sherman's army marching through Scotland County. Because the Union had heard of Cowan's activities throughout South Carolina, they showed very little mercy scavenging and looting all things of value in his family home. The army would hold the Cowan family hostage, taking their livestock, personal possessions, and food, leaving them nothing. An individual soldier who had joined the Union as a deserter of the Confederacy revealed to the Cowans that he was a North Carolinian. The soldier would safeguard the family from any harm as the army looted their home. "As night came on, the guard told my father he must take his family out of that house, for he had to return to camp, and when the rest of the army came up that night he would not answer for the consequences, so after dark, we stole quietly through that camp to an old Temperance Hall about a quarter of a mile away," said Dorset. The family would continue to hide out in a Temperance Hall near Springfield with very few resources until all of Sherman's army had passed through.

According to Caudill, "There were a lot of legends passed down. A fair number of the Confederate officers from the region were Masons. The Masonic Lodge was very big in this area. A lot of these men had given their wives the secret Masonic distress signal. A lot of Sherman's officers were Masons as well. Some houses along the border area were sparred because the wives of these veterans had displayed those Masonic distress signals and might've been treated a little bit better. They attribute that to the Masonic symbolism." A home-fashioned money belt worn by Mary Jane MacLeod Smith of the Wakulla community in Robeson County was meant to conceal money from soldiers in the hopes they wouldn't violate a woman, according to the Scottish Heritage Center. A farm journal maintained by Archibald McEachern of Mill Prong Plantation recounts McEachern's thoughts on Sherman's army passing through Scotland County on March 16, 1865: "One week today since Sherman and his army pranced through our country. He left desolation and ruin on his track. We cannot hear one word from our great General Lee." Parts of Sherman's vast army would also leave their mark on Robeson County.

Sherman's army would eventually be challenged by the Confederates at the Battle of Bentonville, in Johnston County — the largest land battle on North Carolina soil, which resulted in the joining of Union forces under Sherman with those from eastern North Carolina, ultimately preventing a southern retreat from the Confederate forces in Virginia. This all but brought an end to the Civil War." (Jalen Head is a spring intern from The University of North Carolina at Pembroke.)

Battle of Bentonville NC 1865

Johnston County, North Carolina from March 19 - 21, 1865

The Battle of Bentonville was a veritable who's-who of discarded Confederate leaders: Joe Johnston, Braxton Bragg, Lafayette McLaws, Alfred Colquitt, Evander Law, and William B. Taliaferro were just some of the hapless commanders on the field. The 22,000-man army that Johnston commanded looked much more impressive on paper. The army consisted of the remnants of the Army of Tennessee, the Department of North Carolina, and the Department of South Carolina, Georgia, and Florida, with other castoffs joining along the way.

Battle of Averasboro

"In the aftermath of the Battle of Averasboro, William T. Sherman continued his march through the Carolinas, destroying railroads and disrupting supply lines on its way to join General Ulysses S. Grant's army near Petersburg and Richmond. On March 19, 1865, as the respective Federal wings approached Goldsboro, North Carolina, Major General Henry W. Slocum's wing encountered Johnston's hodgepodge army. Johnston's forces concentrated at Bentonville with the hope of falling upon Slocum's wing before the Federal wing of Major General Oliver O. Howard could come to Slocum's support.

Convinced that he faced only a paltry Confederate cavalry force, Slocum launched an attack to disperse them. In turn, the Yankees were driven back. Slocum then established a makeshift defensive line northeast of the Harper house and called for reinforcements. Meantime, Johnston's army arrayed itself to deal a blow to Slocum. It took the Confederates the better part of the day to bring their offensive to life. After 3 p.m., the Rebel line surged forward. Major General Robert F. Hoke's division of the Army of Northern Virginia attacked the right of Slocum's line, driving back Slocum's men and overrunning the Union XIV Corps field hospital. While on the Union left, the remnants of the Confederate Army of Tennessee crashed into the weak Federal line. While many of the Federal units were driven back, Brigadier General James D. Morgan's Union division held out against the onslaught, and eventually, Union reinforcements arrived to support a counterattack. The Confederates reached their high-water mark at the Morris Farm, where Union forces formed a defensive line.

After several Confederate attacks failed to dislodge the Union defenders, the courageous rebels pulled back to their original lines. Nightfall brought the first day's fighting to a close in a tactical draw.

The next day, Howard's right-wing arrived to reinforce Slocum, which put the Confederates at a numerical disadvantage. Sherman expected Johnston to retreat and was inclined to let him do so. Although Johnston began evacuating his wounded, he refused to give up his tenuous position, guarding his only route of escape across Mill Creek. Outnumbered, his only hope for success was to entice Sherman into attacking his entrenched position, something Sherman was unlikely to do.

The next day, Johnston remained in position, and skirmishing resumed. Heavy fighting erupted south of the Goldsboro Road in an area later called the "Bull Pen" between Morgan's and Hoke's men. Under heavy rainfall, Union Major General Joseph A. Mower led a "little reconnaissance" toward the Mill Creek Bridge. When Mower discovered the weakness of the Confederate left flank, Mower launched an attack against the small force holding the bridge. A Confederate counterattack, combined with Sherman's order for Mower to withdraw, ended the advance, allowing Johnston's army to retain control of their only means of supply and retreat. Johnston's men retreated across the bridge that evening, ending the battle. Sherman pursued Johnston's army toward Raleigh—capturing the city on April 13. The war in the Western Theater was ending." On March 13, 1865, a recon patrol of twelve black Union Troops fired near the Basslok family's large Four-thousand-acre tobacco plantation south of Morrisville, North Carolina. In the early morning at 9 am, nine Union troops lay dead and three returned on horseback to Morrisville North Carolina to report to General Judson Kilpatrick that near Fuquay Springs, North Carolina they encountered a well-armed company of North Carolina Confederate irregulars.

"In the late sixteenth century, Sir Walter Raleigh's Roanoke colonists in the region that became North Carolina found that the Native Americans raised tobacco-the Indian's "holy herb"-and that it was smoked by all ages and both genders in clay pipes and used as snuff. The settlers began to grow Indian crops, and in time tobacco became Carolina's leading "money crop" or export to the British Isles and Europe… Tobacco production in North Carolina continued to increase throughout the eighteenth and nineteenth centuries. By 1850 the state was producing approximately 12 million pounds a year, and by 1860 that figure had skyrocketed to 33 million pounds. Part of this increase came as a result of the discovery of a new type of tobacco leaf and a new curing process."

(courtesy of Tobacco by W. W. Yeargin, 2006; Revised November 2022./Additional research provided by Wiley J. Williams.

Basslok Farmlands' Home Development

THE GOOD

Jack Von Dimon was a sixty-three old, retired man who stood at five feet ten inches tall. Jack grew up on Chicago's Southside which was a high-crime area, and he learned basic survival skills. During his four years at Gage Park High School, he was recognized as an achiever as well as an officer in the US Army ROTC (Reserve Officers Training Corp). Jack enjoined the opportunity to learn leadership skills as he was an invert who tried desperately to become an extroverted leader of men in the military. Jack had a sensitive part of his personality as he wrote poetry and played the piano, winning two medals at the Chicago Piano competition. After high school, Jack received help from his parents to enroll at an excellent university.

When Jack finished one year at Bradley University in Peoria Illinois, he enlisted in the United States Air Force. He served in combat along the Laos and Vietnam border areas as a crew chief with an Air America team supporting CIA MACV covert operations against the Viet Cong.

Upon Jack's Honorable Military Discharge, he attempted to continue his degree goals. Jack worked at the Chicago Main US Post Office and studied in the evenings at the local Lyons Township Community College and the University of Illinois Chicago Circle. With his savings, Jack transferred to Northern Illinois University in Dekalb. After graduation, Jack immediately arranged housing in Long Beach California, and moved to work in the Mitsubishi International Trading business. Jack married and with his wife, he moved to Kansas City. Jack was promoted to Regional District Manager for three years. Upon returning to San Francisco California, he began his studies for his master's in international business administration degree. Jack applied himself and achieved high grades. However, his relationship with his wife fell apart. Jack began to realize that he had anger issues and nightmares from his combat experience in Southeast Asia. Jack had disturbing thoughts, feelings, or dreams related to combat events, mental, and physical distress, difficulty sleeping, and changes in how he would think and feel about his personal feelings towards others. Jack was in a constant struggle with himself. Jack married again and had two children, but the relationship fell apart. He moved from stable to unstable relationships. Jack's marriage would last from two to three years, and he would find himself running away. He performed well in his employment but soon the same cycle would begin. Jack returned to the San Francisco Bay Area and sought physical and thought therapy at the Veterans Administration in Palo Alto, California. Over time, the injuries to his legs resulted in the complete replacement of his ankle and hip. Luckily, the VA provide a location for his rehab as he was staying at the time in Redwood City with a woman from Manila Philippines. The neighborhood was run by a Mexican drug gang and soon Jack found himself face to-face with their leader. The encounter resulted in the drug lord having a broken chin and arm. Jack received a broken nose but also gained the respect of the gang. Jack was able to walk the five blocks to the bus stop to travel to Palo Alto each day without being attacked. Jack soon recovered from his surgeries and began a sales marketing career in Silicon Valley. Jack had to be flexible and adaptive as technology would change and he had to reinvent himself to survive. Silicon Vallely grew social media giants like Yahoo, Google, Facebook, and Twitter, and semiconductor firms such as Intel, AMD, and National Semiconductor. Jack Von Dimon loved the intellectual challenges and the constant learning requirements of Silicon Valley. Jack was an adjunct marketing and management professor for over twelve years. Jack received numerous awards for teaching and scholarships.

Then the moment came after two decades when Jack realized that the "Valley" consisted of Monopolies and small innovation firms could no longer thrive. Unionists from San Francisco moved into the area and a construction boom resulted in noise, congestion, and an influx of engineers from India and China who competed for the available American engineering jobs. California became a statewide sanctuary State of illegal Mexicans who would vote for the Communist race-based gay Democratic Party. Churches were closed and people were living on the sidewalks along Camino Real Street in front of Stanford University. Outsourcing of technology then Innovation died but lawyers were like ants who infected businesses, government, and high-tech firms. The joy and challenge were swept aside for "WOKE" political agendas. (The word WOKE became entwined with the Black Lives Matter movement; instead of just being a word that signaled awareness of injustice or racial tension, it became a word of action," according to Merriam-Webster. "Activists were woke and called on others to stay woke.)

Taxes were raised to pay for the social welfare of Joseph Biden's ten million illegals flooding into every corner of life. Crime rose and thus new police administration buildings and jails were built to house them. Jack knew that to be a "freeman," he would have to find sanity and rebirth in another American location.

Go East Californians

In 2015, JACK VON DIMON, first arrived in Raleigh Wake County to explore moving to a peaceful location to write his thoughts and continue the e-publishing business. Before that period, Jack had explored moving to Tampa or Pensacola Florida. Jack flew to those locations from the San Jose California Airport. Jack grew up on a pig and wheat farm in Hamlet Indiana and the vast acreage space of his Polish grandparent's farm led him as a young boy to become extrospective and eager to see the world. Jack's parents moved to Chicago and he was later educated in the State of Illinois. At 18 years of age and eager to see the world, he joined the US Air Force with tours in Japan and Vietnam. Reluctantly returning to the cold weather storms and after receiving a Bachelor of Science in Business Management, he escaped to the warm climate of California and moved to San Francisco to be employed in International Trade.

Jack found the perfect working environment in the diversity of challenges in the Bay Area. Jack was a man of strength and vision who prospered in the High Technology Silicon Valley for close to two decades. Over time, the city of Mountain View California went from a peaceful artist town along the Northern California Peninsula to a large congested city of campuses of the billion-dollar social media and Semiconductor Technology giants such as Google, Facebook, Twitter, Intel, and AMD. State, County, and City Taxes soared while the quiet software development environment became an apex of traffic noise and high rents. Jack was thrown into despair as he watched how the dynamic startup venture capital businesses became top-down monopoly corporate structures that reached across the State, America, and the World. This man enjoyed the learning challenges of being a Technology Marketing Manager. It was intense but before the trillion-dollar company complexes, it was quite an opportunity to meet engineers and managers who later became legends, such as Steve Wozniak and Steve Jobs. Then Jack's world collapsed.

Each morning, Jack would wake up at 9 am in his rental home in the Santa Cruz Mountains of California. Now, with the overbuilt housing sector in Silicon Valley, he had to get ready to drive Highway 9 snaked through the Santa Cruz Mountains to meet some clients for investment funding. If Jack did not leave by 9 am, the long line of cars driving to Silicon Valley would be impossible to endure. The continual daily process of leaving early and returning to his rental home in Santa Cruz, no later than 1:30 pm, was taking a toll on the execution of his company startup funding. The window for driving on the congested highway was short. Jack spent two and half hours driving and accomplishing nothing. If he left the Valley after 3 pm, the drive home would be slow and difficult. After a long career as an entrepreneur and a university academic, Jack had enough and decided to leave California. Where could he move to? Could Jack find his dream home that would be free from construction and vehicle noises? Well, like all of Jack's dreams, they came true, but they did not last long.

A Perfect Dream Home in NC Wake County

Jack Von Dimon's career was as a systems analyst and business planner and did not believe in living a stress-filled existence. So, he set up appointments with several real estate agents in Florida and North Carolina. Once appointments were made and confirmed, he would fly to the three locations; namely, Tampa, Pensacola, and Raleigh, that satisfied his "dream home" criteria. Jack Von Dimon spent three months meeting many dishonest and only commission-seeking agents. Jack visited a total of twenty-seven homes. He was frustrated as none of his goals were reached, but then he met an angel and honest real estate agent, her name was Molly. Molly was enthusiastic and sincere in realizing the ideal home that Jack was seeking. She was an attractive blonde who stood five feet and six inches in height. She achieved her real estate license after receiving her diploma from North Carolina University, two years after graduating from High School in Cary North Carolina. Molly was married to her high school sweetheart, George Bonaro, and had a fourteen-year-old daughter, Maria. Molly had great discipline and business skills and was always focused on achieving Jack's need to find a home in a quiet rural area with a forest area that was within a cul-de-sac.

The lender was slow in responding and called Molly on March 8, 2018, at 9 am, "Molly, I understand where everyone is coming from, but like you and I have discussed multiple times, asking us to close in three weeks puts us a lender in a very, very difficult spot. Again, the file hasn't even been submitted yet as we don't have the initial closing disclosures back. I understand we have the appraisal, but if and when we get the file initially submitted, we're still well behind the 8-ball. Everyone won't care about the initial delay multi-week delay, they'll only care about closing on time and we as the lender will feel the brunt of everyone being upset about where we are in the process and why this file can't be rushed to the front of the line at every stage of our process. I'm not saying that it can't be done but again, it's just very, very unlikely but not having the file submitted in the next day or two will make it impossible."

The process was lengthy covering over five months as Jack Von Dimon would fly from San Jose California to Raleigh North Carolina each month to review homes that Molly had selected. In the third month, Jack and Molly agreed on a one-story home, three bedrooms, and two baths with one acre of land within a Homeowners Association run of eighty Mungo Homes.

The negotiations with the current owners were skillfully administered by Molly and her team. With her sincere efforts to maintain the desires and cost as dictated by Jack, the deal was completed with a Mortgage firm that catered to US Military Veterans. Jack signed amendments to the close date of 4/13/2018, but in the world of finance, the actual mortgage was completed in July 2018. Jack signed amendments to the close date of 4/13/2018, but in the world of finance, the actual mortgage was completed in July 2018. In California, Jack prepared to leave for Raleigh, and only after he was forced to sign over 100 documents.

"Damn it Jim, who was Jack's business partner, I thought buying a home would be easy. Ok, this is done but my hip and ankle are increasing in pain. I sure hope, Molly, that this does not slow me down. Thanks again for all your help. You are the greatest. Take care see you soon." Jack hung up the phone and took a beer from the refrigerator, sat down, placed his feet on his office desk, and relaxed. The final period he thought to have finally reached his moment of happiness.

Jack now had to arrange moving and his basic furniture. On August 15, 2018, Jack arrived at an air flight that landed at RDU. He stayed at the Fuquay Varina hotel for two weeks so he could purchase a new Toyota SUV and order a mattress and some basic linens. It was a dream he realized and was eager to meet his three neighbors.

Jack was anxious to meet his neighbors. Before August 2018, his neighbor walked across the road and introduced himself. He was a powerful man with a cheerful smile. This exchange gave Jack hope that all his neighbors had the same attitude and willingness to be friends. Jack had no idea that he was to meet two neighbors from Hell and one from Heaven.

On August 21, 2018, Jack was experiencing unbearable pain from his joint injuries from the Vietnam War in his left hip and ankle. Jack had the Durham VA outsource both Jack Von Dimon's hip and ankle replacements to EmergeOrtho due to its high number of medical professionals. Jack met and interviewed extremely competent Surgeons; namely, Dr. Nickolas A. Viens, MD, and Michael K. Merz, MD. Jack felt extremely pleased and knew that his outcome would be positive.

Jack's left hip was removed and replaced on September 20, 2018, at 9 am by Dr. Merz. Jack spent three days in the Emerge-Ortho Durham Hospital.

After three months, Jack finally was able to see Dr. Vienz and he approved going ahead with the ankle surgery as his recent hip would not be an issue. Jack learned on September 16, 2019, that Jack's "cast for his left ankle" was not made, but a current x-ray needed to be taken.

Jack Von Dimon told Dr. Merz, "Doctor I live alone. I am new to the area. I have no friends in Raleigh to help me after I return home from my surgery. My home has a steep driveway. Therefore, I will be isolated. I cannot understand why. Could you please arrange for in-home care at your end or some contact point here? Who will change the bedding, prepare meals, help shower, do laundry help, and do some errands that I might need? I have no contact point except Walter Jenkins, Durham VA ER, on the 1st floor, F-wing." Dr. Merz said, "Do not worry Jack, I am calling the VA for the Well-Care Home Health Agency to arrive at your home at the same time we discharge you and have our transportation bring you home."

Jack arrived home and Well-Care never arrived. Because Jack had no crutches or mobile scooter devices, Jack had to get on his knees and crawl through the front door of the home within Basslok's Plantation. In addition, he would crawl to the bathroom and hoist himself up onto the toilet set. The refrigerator had no food. For the weekend, Jack did not eat and was forced to sleep on the Living Room Carpet. On Tuesday, a caregiver, Riveria arrived who was Jack's age and could not help with the shower and lifting him into bed. Maria was an illegal Mexican citizen who walked across the Mexican Border cooks and makes only tacos and a salad.

Jack had two major surgeries and his rehabilitation took over nine months, but he never gave up on his dream. Jack was determined to walk again and refocus on his writing and publishing career. In 2019, Jack joined CORA. a local physical therapy office. Tim Mertz was a highly trained MPT. Tim helped Jack Von Dimon to overcome the challenges of hip and ankle removal and replacement physical rehabilitation. Tim gave Jack that pain no longer existed for Jack's life.

THE EVIL

Early Childhood

Jubal Johnson's Great Grand Father Samuel Johnson fought in a local Confederate battle in Goldsboro. North Carolina from 1860 to 1864. Samuel's son Harold was the father of Jubal. The Johnson clan were southern sharecroppers, who lived in wooden shacks and later in inexpensive home trailers. Jubal was aggressive and would bully other boys and especially his brother, Mathew. Jubal would beat up his brother who weighed only 85 lbs. Jubal stood five feet ten inches and was physically strong at 195 lbs.

Jubal received a new Honda motorcycle from his father. Jubal had a wild streak and rode his motorcycle around Morrisville North Carolina without caring about the safety of others. Soon, Jubal was arrested for reckless speeding and attacking a police officer who pulled him over. After sixty days in Jail, Jubal is released but returns after he assaults a seventeen-year-old high school girl as she was standing at a local stop waiting for the eleven am bus. Jubal stopped his motorcycle and walked over. "Hi, how about riding on my cycle? You might have a great time?" Without hesitation, the teenager, Sherry Lawson, said, "NO, get away I would never let you touch me." Jubal became angry and punched her in the face and attempted to rape her, but a passing police officer stopped and rushed to Sherry's aid, and placed Jubal in handcuffs. Jubal was nineteen and would find himself back in jail for twelve months for assault. He expressed no remorse during the trial and was on probation for twenty-four more months.

Jubal had no feelings, and he was a psychopath. He demonstrated every human psychopathic tendency that would appear normal but with a lack of remorse and consciousness. He lacked empathy with other people for they simply are objects to be used. Cocaine would make him delusional and paranoid.

Volunteer Fireman

After Jubal's convictions were quashed by the Raleigh Superior Court, he worked in local construction jobs and when he was 23, he volunteered to be a local fireman. For two years, Jubal did not see much action. So, over discussions at the Aviator with his group of 7 volunteer firefighters, who ranged in age from 17 to 42, they conspire to set fires to abandoned buildings and wooded areas in rural Johnson County North Carolina. They went about setting a dozen fires that were deliberately set. They then called in the fire and then rushed to put out the fire. They were featured in the Johnstonian News as courageous firefighters heroes. Jubal received a commendation letter and an award of 5,000 dollars.

Woman of Intelligence – Cathy Ireland Durhman

At 28, Cathy Ireland Durhman is a petite blonde who is 96 lbs of pure sexual beauty. Cathy is the only daughter of her parents who work for IBM. She is raised in Rockville New York State and loves journalism, swimming, and sports. Cathy develops a keen interest in sports medicine after her high hero and sweetheart, Jim Bezmak, breaks his neck in a football game. Doctors believe that it is the result of the Riddell Football Helmet. Jim, and Cathy never had a long-term relationship. Jim is to remain in for the rest of his life in a wheelchair. After high school, Cathy focuses on obtaining an education within the journalism field. Upon receiving her B.A. degree, she developed an interest in physical therapy for athletes. Two years passed and she enrolled in a master's degree program at Rockville University and interned as a Physical Therapist at the Regional Clinic. Doctors and patients love her. Cathy is a happy positive woman who cares about her patients. Cathy moves to North Carolina to take a position as a Physical Therapist Coordinator at the Durham Emerge Ortho Surgery Hospital. In the evening, she begins a degree in Special Education at Semi College. Due to the economic slowdown in her profession, Cathy interviewed for a teacher position in elementary education. Ultimately, it comes to pass that Cathy Ireland Durhman loves children. She has a wild streak and loves motorcycles and drags racing with her Pontiac Trans Sport. On a drinking holiday, she meets a handsome athletic man, Jubal Johnson. Their connection was love at first sight. After spending time together at racing events and tooling around the coastline of the Carolinas. -one year later they marry in a chapel within Harrah's Cherokee Casino Resort. With Cathy's savings and her mother's 401K balance, they move into a Factory Expo two-bedroom, one-bathroom home trailer. Within two years, they have two beautiful boys named Bobbie and

Johnnie Johnson. Cathy continues to work as an elementary teacher and only takes two weeks of maternity leave. They are a loving family and plan to buy a larger home when the boys are five and six years of age.

Husband and Father – Jubal Johnson

At 38 years old, Jubal Johnson stood at five feet 11 inches tall. He had a stocky built from working out daily at the Fit-4-Life Cleveland Gym. Jubal was all muscle at 185 lbs. His normal attire was a colored t-shirt, Outdoor Softshell Fleece Lined Cargo Pants Snow Ski Hiking Pants with Belt containing a silver Cowboy buckle. Jubal wore Wolverine Floorhand Waterproof 6" Steel Toe Work Boots that gave him an extra two inches of height. He walked with an aggressive Durham gang member swagger.

Jubal had applied for the U.S. Marine Corps in Fayetteville, but after four months was discharged for fighting in the barracks. Jubal did not fit into a regimented organization and he preferred to make his own rules. As he said to his drill sergeant, "It is my way or the highway for you." When the sergeant demanded that Jubal get down and do 100 push-ups, Jubal hit the sergeant in the chin. The blow caused the sergeant to respond with orders from other members of the platoon to grab Jubal and tie him up. Jubal was in the brig for two days and was discharged for the convenience of the Marine Corps.

Jubal returned home and said nothing about why he decided to leave the Marines. After that, he worked three construction jobs and continued to be a volunteer firefighter. He had an explosive temper and disciplined his sons by roping them to their beds if they do not listen or bed wetting. After work, he and his workmates meet at Carpenter sports bar and return home at 11 pm. On many weekend occasions, Jubal gets drunk around the home. In 2015, on Christmas eve, he arrives home in a taxi. He is happy and has gifts for the Christmas tree. Cathy asks where he has been since 6 pm. Jubal turns towards his wife and shouts, "Damn it. I am the man around this house. No woman is going to question me!" He rushes Cathy and throws her to the carpet and slaps her violently.

Jubal then stood up and kicked her. "This should teach you a lesson." His sons awakened and ran into the living room screaming. "Mommy, Mommy what happened." Jubal then looks at his two boys and snaps! "Mommy and Daddy are fine. Now, get to bed or Santa is not going to come."

Jubal takes off his belt and threatens the boys with a beating. Bobby and Johnnie ran back crying into their bedroom. The next day, Cathy takes the boys, while Jubal is sleeping off his drunken rage. She spends Christmas with her mother.

Jubal arrives later and pleads, " I was wrong to have acted that way and to come back home. I will never harm you or the boys. "

After two weeks, Cathy returns. Jubal has grand plans as he is getting a managerial job with a boat Marine motor company at a great salary. "Cathy lets us buy a new home to start a new life with the boys. We can buy a new five-bedroom home that has a yard for the boys, and you can also have an office for studies and part-time employment. I can work on building a great playground and a fenced-in area for our dogs. It is going to be a real heaven for all of us." Cathy begins to cry. "Jubal, I remember how we did things that were crazy when we first met. Now, we need to settle down peacefully and raise our boys in a quiet and safe neighborhood. I love you." Within two years, they have the funds for a mortgage on the home of their dreams. Jubal keeps secret the source of his savings for a home. Jubal sells cocaine and fentanyl to his firefighter friends and establishes a street drug dealer network in Durham and Algiers.

New Home and Changed Circumstances

Jubal and Cathy buy a home in a Private Community located in the former farmlands of the Basslok family. The two-story home consists of 4 bedrooms, 3 baths, and 2500sq.feet with a backyard of one acre. The backyard is open, and neighbors share an open forest-like atmosphere.

However, after one year, Jubal has a difficult time controlling his temper and his drinking. Jubal physically struggles with his wife. Jubal's wife has bruise marks on her arms and face. Cathy's mother notices her distress and asks what is happening.

"Mom, Jubal is a hard-working provider but spends his money drinking with his friends and buying them gifts and dinners. He gives me little money for groceries and refuses clothing for our sons. The boys have no new shoes or even underwear. He believes that he has a right to take care of his wife as he decides. I don't know what to do!"

Four weeks later, Cathy and Jubal agree to see a Marriage Counselor. After four months of sessions, Jubal agrees to stop drinking. However, he takes up the habit of smoking marijuana. This appears to work, and he is calm. His anger outburst is redirected to his construction activities at their home. Jubal drinks secretly with his firefighters but before going home always has coffee and smokes a joint.

Soon Jubal begins to design his major construction projects without notification of his neighbors or the local HOA (Home Owners Association). He begins arguments over his neighbors' trees, grass lengths, and insects at the local children's play area. When neighbors place Christmas lighting that is to grandeur than his decorations, at night he cuts the electrical wires and sits in the top stair window to see what their reaction will be. In Jubal's mind, all the land belongs to him as he is lord and master of an estate. Soon, neighbors begin to view Jubal as an evil guy who gets "kicks out of" harming others in the neighborhood. Soon, Jubal places floodlights on his home as he is concerned that the home will be burglarized. Jubal has two large bulldogs that roam freely and terrorized his neighbor's collie. Wake County animal control arrives many times to separate the dogs and place an order for Jubal to control them or build some sort of containment. Jubal erects a six-foot wood fence around his property line and begins to build a large swimming pool on a slope.

The (HOA) community manager, Mrs. Lightfoot, inspects the property and points out some violations. "Jubal, your swimming pool is not authorized and further you laid the foundation on a 25% downward angle. It is sure to slide during rainstorms. I think you will have to remove it or pay a penalty of $10,000." Jubal's face was turning red when he heard her statement. "This is my property and you can tell me what to do with it!" Mrs. Lightfoot felt that the way Jubal approached her that her safety was being threatened. "Jubal, I see you have strong feelings. Let me have a meeting with our local HOA. I am sure we can work things out." Mrs. Lightfoot, without further comment, walked swiftly out of the cluttered backyard and ran to her car. She felt her hands sweating and a tightening of her chest. Once the car started, she looked out the side window and saw Jubal Johnson walking outside with a hammer. She put the Mercedes in gear and raced down the hill. Mrs. Lightfoot had saved her life and would not lose it over some damn swimming pool of a crazy person.

THE BAD

Gabe Preston was born on February 12, 1978, and grew up in Sharpsburg Maryland a small town of 350 with a history of the American Civil War. Thousands of Irish and German immigrants used the Sharpsburg route of the wagon roads traveling from Pennsylvania as far south as North Carolina.

Gabe's great-grandfather, Westly Preston, was a hero of the Battle of Antietam. Westly lived with his parents and seven brothers on a 600-acre farm growing wheat and tobacco. In 1860, upon reaching the age of seventeen, Westly became a cavalry officer in the Army of Northern Virginia. Westley's only son, Sean Preston, left the farm at fifteen and moved with a traveling circus to North Carolina.

Courtesy of the Sharpsburg NC (Battle of Antietam)

"Confederate General Robert E. Lee invaded Maryland with his Army of Northern Virginia in the summer of 1862 and was intercepted near the city by Union General George B. McClellan with the Army of the Potomac. The rival armies met on September 17, 1862, in the Battle of Antietam (also called the Battle of Sharpsburg). It would be the bloodiest single day in all American military annals, with a total of nearly 23,000 casualties to both sides. A few days earlier, the multi-sited Battle of South Mountain occurred at the three low-lying passes in South Mountain—Crampton's Gap, Turner's Gap, and Fox's Gap—where Lee's forces attempted to hold back the advancing Union regiments moving westward, especially along the important National Road (now U.S. Route 40 Alternate) which is now a part of South Mountain State Battlefield Park.

Major Westly Preston led his cavalry of fifty men under intense fire from Union Forces, to capture McClellan's armed cavalry battalion. In addition, when he was shot and fell off his mount, he rallied his troops to take a stand near South Mountain, killing 179 Black Union troops. Wesley fought on until General Lee ordered a retreat back across Antietam Creek. Although bleeding from his wounds, Westly continued to fire upon the Union soldiers until all of his men were safe across the Creek. When Wesley had his wounds cared for in the Richmond military hospital, he would return to his family farm in 1865 with one leg amputated. The Preston home was used as a firing location for Union forces and its roof was destroyed and their owned slaves were gone. In the years following the influx of black carpet baggers, Westly was given recognition for his bravery with the Sons of the Confederacy, and he joined the KKK. In 1868, Westly married Maria Murphy and they had three girls and one son, Sean Preston.

"The drawn battle is considered a turning point of the war since it kept the Confederacy from winning a needed victory on Northern soil, which might have gained it European recognition. Lee's retreat gave Abraham Lincoln the opportunity he needed to issue his Emancipation Proclamation, declaring all slaves residing in rebelling Confederate territory against the federal government, to be free. This act made it even more unlikely that Europe would grant diplomatic recognition to the South."

Courtesy of the War Memorial Washington DC (Union General George B. McClellan with the Army of the Potomac.

Sean Preston stood at six foot three inches at 21 years of age. After three years of taking care of the six Bengal tigers and five elephants of the Barnum Circus and traveling across the Carolinas, he met a Scottish woman, Beth MacLeod, at a local tavern in Cabarrus County. Sean bought a Barley Tobacco farm of 100 acres. Burley tobacco grows well due to a favorable climate marked by moderate temperatures with high relative humidity and soil types suitable for nutrient retention. Shortly after six months of marriage, Sean and Beth, had two twin sons, Gabe and Robert.

The boys grew up under the strict rules of their father Sean. They learned about the heroes of the Confederacy and posted the Confederate Flag in their bedrooms. When the boys were sixteen, they were given confederate rifles by their father. Sean told his sons about their grandfather and his courageous actions at Sharpsburg. The Preston family grew to hate the Union and anyone from the "North." During a hunting trip using shotguns, Robert was walking in front of Gabe as they crossed the wood area near their farm, several pheasants flew up, and Gabe fired immediately, hitting Robert in the back of the head. Gabe ran towards Robert. "Robert, are you alright? Damn, I did not see you. I was just shooting at the birds. Get up and stop pretending." Robert lay on his back and Gabe noticed that blood was on the grass. Robert's eyes were closed, and blood was also tripping out of his mouth. Gabe turned him around and noted small holes in his skull and neck.

Gabe panicked and ran back to the farm and upon arriving rushed into the barn where Sean was drying tobacco leaves. "Dad, Robert got hurt. We were hunting and he ran in front of me. I think he needs some help." Sean got on his horse and reached out his hand for Gabe to jump up on the back of the horse. They raced for thirty minutes. When they arrived at the still body of Robert, Sean could see the blood from his son's back. "Gabe, stay here and lift Robert on the horse and I will race to the town's clinic. I am sure he will be fine and do not worry. Accidents happen."

At 3 pm, a County Sheriff's cruiser arrived with Sean and Beth, at the location where Robert's blood still was wet on the grass, Gabe was smoking a "joint" and crying. Sean spoke with tears in his eyes as he held his hand of Beth, "You killer, you murdered your brother. I trained with clear rules on how to hunt and respect the use of firearms. The Deputy believes you did this on purpose. You might go to jail today. So why did you kill him?" Gabe spoke, "Dad, even if he was stupid, I loved my twin brother. We fought before going hunting today but would never harm him over that."

Gabe spent two years in juvenile detention until he was eighteen and returned to the family for probation of five years, or twenty-three years of age. Sean never could forgive Gabe for what he did. The Carpetbag Black Criminal Court Judge ruled that it was an accident that he had planned but with dimension capacity.

Gabe found living under the daily strict control of his father, Sean, difficult. To escape the daily pain of the lack of freedom, he began to use moonshine whiskey and Cannabis. His anger against his father was transferred to the Civil War and all "Northerners" as what happened to him. His personality would range from normal calm, but once he drank, he would become aggressive. If he entered a bar, he would take issue immediately with males who he thought were "northerners." So, without hesitation, he would walk up to his targeted male, and punch him until they fell to the floor. Then Gabe would walk out of the bar and jump on his motorcycle and disappear.

Over time, Gabe and his parents kept the family secrets that he killed his brother and lacked social interest. Since the death of his brother, he hated socializing and would avoid eye-to-eye contact. Even if someone reached out to him as he had an impressive appearance of an athlete, Gabe would avoid responding. Gabe stood at 6 feet 4 inches. -Wore tight pants, t-shirts, cowboy boots, short crew-cut hair, and always clean-shaven. Gabe was a basketball player for his high school but never had any ambition to become an NBA player, although he could become great and was scouted by Duke University as extremely talented.

Since the death of Robert, Gabe Preston had an attitude toward his "Southern-born privilege wealthy classes" when none existed. Gabe lived in an imaginary world where he hated and would beat up his father plus all "Northerners". Gabe loved his father but in his delusionary nightmares wanted him dead for not protecting him from imprisonment. In those dreams, he imagined Sean having a rope around his neck that had worms eating his face.

After working in the Financial Services Industry as an associate manager at First Citizens Bank, Gabe studied in the evenings and received an Associate of Arts degree in Real Estate. In his class at the University of North Carolina, he was attracted to a beautiful five-foot 5inches woman from Connecticut.

Mary Beth Gladstone

After meeting with her for dinner dates and introducing Mary Beth Gladstone to his dad Sean and mother, Gabe and Mary Beth continued to date. Gabe had many fears about being intimate with anyone. but Mary Beth was a warm and loving woman. Mary Beth was a delicate woman at five feet and four inches. With blue eyes and a creamy white complexion, she immediately attracted men. She had a large amount of brown hair that she dyed blonde. She was cheerful as a child. Her mother died 12 years after Mary Beth was born. Her father moved to Charlotte North Carolina after accepting a position as Vice President of Global Financial Operations. Mary Beth was married to a business partner in the real estate company she worked at. The marriage was annulled when she discovered that he was stealing the commission on home sales of his associates. He would hire them and upon their selling a home, which would take two months for the home to sell, he would fire them based on some contrived violation and pocket the commission. May Beth quit and moved on to become a five-star revenue generator at Coldwell Banker.

Love Blossoms

During loving moments with Mary Beth, Gabe soon let down his defenses and told her what happened in his life. The revelation led to trust between them and soon Gabe decided to ask Mary Beth Gladstone for her hand in marriage. Mary Beth revealed that she could never have children as she wanted to protect the planet. Gabe agreed that as a baby would only complicate their life. Still, Mary Beth yearned for a family that she and Gabe could surround their love with.

On a beautiful summer day, they were married in Myrtle Beach South Carolina. They did not tell anyone, they just wanted privacy. To them, this was a new life and Gabe could leave his delusions and moments when he would become aggressive with no warning, and people would not consider him dangerous. Mary Beth was a clear thinker and not a psychological woman who had no belief that she was being harassed or being caught up in a catastrophic event. The couple was perfect, they shared mutual strength, and both had a right to become wealthy and buy a home. Mary Beth encouraged Gabe to expand his career in Finance but when he was offered a six-figure income to work with Chase Bank in Charlotte, he became destructive and did not have a positive image of himself, so his mind went back to a simple life in which he did not need to socialize. Gabe needed to stop reliving the killing of his brother, Robert Preston. However, Mary Beth Preston needed her husband to not only be her protector and lover but to be active in socializing within the North Carolina trillion-dollar real estate sales Industry.

After selling their first home in Charlotte, Mary Beth found a home in a forest area that had an (HOA) Homeowners Association that was looking for new buyers and a paid director of this property located in Garner North Carolina. The home was one story with three acres of land facing a forest area. Gabe fantasized that he would finally live on a farm like his father's property and his grandfather's. Mary Beth had the financial resources after Gabe's father refused to extend a loan. On an April 2012 day, they signed all the documents and moved into their love home. Gabe's mother had a close attraction to Gabe after Robert's killing.

After his first meeting with Mary Beth, Gabe saw her as the mother he never had. Mothers do not have their son's babies. Mary Beth also had no babies.

With Mary Beth's lack of knowledge, Gabe found a source of Cannabis and began secretly on the back of their property, to drink strong whiskey. Gabe did not take any jobs that would benefit the couple's funds instead he joined the low-paying HOA position and would take loans from his father, Sean. Gabe loved working outside and viewed himself as a typical Southern Confederate who loved farming and logging. So, he began to cut his trees until his home stood as an island of weeds with no beauty except a place for his three trucks and five dogs.

The Garner neighbors see Mary Beth working each day as she dashed out to meet Sales to close Real Estate clients in her black corvette. Gabe's wife wore no bra clothing, loose, and her pantsuits were expensive and professional.

Mary Beth Preston spent her quiet times planting flowers and wanting order in her life which consisted of crying secretly during her first four years of marriage smoking Cannabis with Gabe and doing lines of cocaine that no one in the neighborhood ever suspected. Mary Beth was a kind loving woman versus her husband smokes cannabis and drink whiskey with the local neighbors until his hostility emerges. He becomes angry, screaming and shouting at his best friends until he leaves with Mary Beth. Gabe then refuses to socialize again. During their sexual naked experiences, Mary Beth knows how to use sex and control to calm Gabe's period of paranoia due to excessive smoking and nightly whiskey bottles. In 2020, the ambitious, perfect, and smart Preston couple resolved to start again and become millionaires in Real Estate in North Carolina. Gabe and Mary Beth were perfect. Gabe became confident under the umbrella of Mary Beth's love and control. Gabe adored her but within his mind, she was outperforming him financially and making him into a small little boy as his mother did after Robert died. Gabe struggled with these feelings every day and with his new German Shephard, he placed his tender tensions upon the dog. So, a barrier with the dog created an invisible fence to eliminate Mary Beth in a nightmare vision of a shallow grave behind their property.

Gabe had multiple personalities. When Jack arrived, he and Gabe became friends as Jack saw a young man in his late 30s who could run for a political office. The HOA viewed him as a leader, and he was respected as a man who was fair and balanced in his decisions. Gabe helped Jack when he struggled to walk and do yard work from serious ankle and hip replacements. Jack appreciated Gabe's help mowing the lawn, planting trees, and removing branches from severe windstorms.

On August 4, 2019, Jubal Johnson called Gabe Preston about a terrible act against the HOA (SAC) that Jack Von Dimon was watering his trees near Jubal's fence. Gabe crossed the property line and rushed towards Jack, "Stop watering as you are going to cause rot on Jubal's. He is angry and complaining. I want to keep him in good spirits." Jack turned off the water and was perplexed. He could not get out of his head that he thought Gabe was a friendly neighbor and faithful friend. It was illogical. When it rains Jubal's fence gets wet and it does rain a lot in North Carolina. Jack did not need Gabe to validate him. This was a false premise that if some of my water touched Jubal's fence it would magically rot, but when God gave rain, it would not rot.

So, Gabe made me a monster Northerner and victim to please Jubal who at this point was running a 24x7 construction zone in his backyard. Gabe showed Jack no respect and treated him with contempt at that moment. Jack Von Dimon resolved never to be his friend or his wife's. Jack released the lesson; namely, never be friends with these southern-born men for they will eventually tell him as a new homeowner from the Yankee North; how to live and think. At that moment, Jack resolved never to respond to fools and mentally bipolar hate-filled neighbors.

When Jack found that could not close the garage door as he would have to climb a ladder to reach the switch. Jack knew that after his hips and ankles were removed and replaced with metal, he stood a 90% chance of falling.- Replacement surgery is extremely dangerous. In addition, he had to close the door to prevent burglaries.

On December 18, 2020, Jack knew that Gabe, who stood over six feet tall, that Gabe could simply climb the ladder and pull the switch. Gabe was in his yard doing some yard work. Jack asked, Hi Gabe, can you please help me pull down the switch on my garage door? I am afraid that I might fall. I believed in our renewed friendship. Gabe stared at Jack Von Dimon. First, ignoring Jack's pleadings and words of fear.

Then Gabe marched over, glaring at Jack, "Look, I am not your slave! I am tired of helping you! You are not my friend. Leave me alone and my wife as well. Never set foot on my property or you will be shot!" Jack knelt and replied, "What, I never thought of you as my slave but as my friend. This is pure bullshit! What is wrong with you.?" Gabe said nothing, just standing a few feet from Jack in a stance to attack. Mary Beth was screaming at Gabe, "What are you doing? What is wrong with you that you cannot help a neighbor in distress who has implants?". Gabe went back into his home as his wife was upset about Gabe's behavior.

Jack was hurt immensely. Was that Southern trait of hating Northerners and was he viewed as a "Carpetbagger?" Even two weeks later when Gabe said he was drinking whiskey and apologized for his words and actions. The die was cast, and Jack would never trust or respect his other southern neighbors. Gabe and Jubal became two evil strange personality bookends. Jack was afraid for his wife who was preparing to visit and start their life in North Carolina. Would Gabe and Jubal attempt to harm his wife or fire upon them when they were sleeping? Jack took his shotgun, rifle, and handguns out the next day and cleaned and oiled each weapon. Jack again was back in Vietnam protecting his foxhole outpost at the Nha Trang Air Base.

PEACEMAKERS

Halldor Josphus

"Blessed are the peacemakers, for they will be called children of God." Jesus -Sermon on the Mount

Halldór Josephus was muscular at six feet and 2 inches in height. Halldór Josephus was raised in Iceland, which has a history of a harsh climate, and animal products dominate Icelandic cuisine. Halldor with an IQ of 150 skips two grades and is placed in a special mathematics and engineering class. He secretly has a dream to migrate to America to begin a career in technology. His hobby is photography focusing on magazine female models. On the weekends, he plays soccer at the local league in Reykjavík. He loves people and is charismatic that naturally leads others to enjoy his company.

Halldor enjoys barbequing and cooking Icelandic cuisine of lamb, dairy, and fish. For family and friends he cooks skyr, hangikjöt (smoked lamb), kleinur, laufabrauð, and bollur. Þorramatur is a traditional buffet that he and his wife Sophie serve at midwinter festivals called Þorrablót; it includes a selection of traditionally cured meat and fish products served with rúgbrauð (dense dark and sweet rye bread) and brennivín (an Icelandic akvavit). The flavors of Icelandic food originated in its preservation methods; pickling in fermented whey or brine, drying, and smoking. When Halldor cooks for special occasions, he emphasizes ingredients produced in Iceland. During neighbor holiday dinners with Jack Von Dimon,

Holldor is proud of the quality of the lamb meat, seafood, and skyr. moss, wild mushrooms, wild thyme, lovage, angelica, and dried seaweed, as well as a wide array of dairy products.

Before moving to North Carolina with his teenage wife and young children, they live in Fairbanks Alaska where his uncle is president of the hundred-million-dollar logging company, Baxter Lumber Mills. Halldor is hired as Baxter's Chief Information Officer. The climate is like Iceland and both parents enjoy the outdoors. They snowmobile in winter and hike in the summer. Halldor goes on hunting and fishing trips with his friends. Sophie does not enjoy living in a tent and the vast number of mosquitoes in the summer.

They are so happy enjoying their children and living in Alaska's economy during the oil boom. They both decide to move to America's Southern Region after Hallbor is offered an excellent lucrative salary. Sophie knows that the children will have a better opportunity in North Carolina and agree that this will be great for the twins and Halldor's job.

At 41ys of age, Halldor works at Raleigh Triangle at Honeywell as a manager of Systems Engineering. His managers and engineers enjoy working with him as he always has a positive attitude and is a commitment to the biblical values of the Roman Catholic Church.

Sophie Josephus

Sophie weighed 95 lbs, had a height of 5 feet, and six inches, and had an athletic body, with a waist of 25 inches. Her body consisted of sculptured soft curves hips, shoulders, and firm breasts. Her eyes were blue, sensual lips, and full-length Germanic shoulder blonde hair. Sophie had a great family and enjoyed meeting new people, cooking, and ballroom dancing. After attending a private school in Bavaria, Sophie was a Lufthansa Airlines stewardess for several years before meeting Halldór at a four-star hotel that was featuring models from Germany. At 18, Sophie, after meeting Halldor as the Der Spiegel photographer at a photo shoot in Reykjavík, fell in love and looked forward to starting a family. Halldor had a dream of a new career in America. Sophie did not want to leave Bavaria and her family. Love was strong between them and she loved this young and energetic man. She then dedicated her life to being together.

At 38, living in North Carolina, Sophie is the ruler behind the throne in her household. Her parents were from Bohemia and Hungary, and despite her husband being elected a senior manager with a major American Company in the North Carolina Raleigh Triangle, she ruled the home and was an important example to her two twin daughters, namely, Sarah and Eve. She followed the Roman Catholic Religion and entered the convent at the age of 15yrs of age and left at 18 seeking a family life. Her historical family roots were traced back to Anna of Bavaria, Queen of the Romans whose husband was Rudolf II, Duke of Bavaria. After the end of WW2, her family's mountain mansion was destroyed by British bombers and the American Army's Expeditionary Forces' Administration that appropriated all bank accounts of German citizens to inflict maximum pain on Germans who voted for Adolph Hitler, a corporal in WW1. Sophie's family was destitute and set out to survive under the Russian and American occupation regulations. Thanks to assets in gold bars, the family survived. In 1945, her father was appointed a Judge of the Nuremberg Trials. Sophie's family was not in the Nazi Socialist Party as they were of German Nobility.

At her American home, Sophie had the presence of a queen and dressed in beautiful flowing gowns with spiked shoes when entering her husband's professional associates. In the home, classical music from

Germany was heard from digital internet radio stations. The home was serene and peaceful. In the evening, before retiring, she and her husband with the two twin girls read poetry from German and Icelandic authors.

HOA - Financial Tyranny

John Rock was a six-figure CEO of the HOA (SAC) Inc. He had over nineteen years of managing all types of Florida, and Carolina Single Family, Townhome, Condominium, and Timeshare Associations. He had a Certified Manager of Community Associations, (CMCA), Association Management Specialist (AMS), and Professional Community Association Manager (PCAM). The Rock family husband and wife team founded SAC in 1975 and incorporated in 1998. In 2021, revenues reach ten million dollars and profits and expansion soars. John Rock hires an attorney, George Daggett, to brow-beat any homeowner who has a complaint relating to (SAC)'s expenses and billing.

Like any company that has poor management that focuses on its cash flow instead of focusing on its people, teamwork declines and bright Wake University graduates soon leave. Under President Rock, he delegated the management of properties to low-paid, unskilled hires. (SAC) property management begins to decline in 2022 with its refusal to honor its agreements. This property management company is a joke, and delays repairs in an untimely manner. In some homes, raw sewage flows on bottom-floor apartments. Homeowners' Associate Members complain about roofs not being repaired and resulting in water damage. Maintenance or management never shows up. Some ceilings have roaches and entry points for rats. Mr. Rock and his wife produce an advertising Video as they sit in front of a Pinehurst mansion. "We believe that an association should function as both a community and a business to meet the expectations of its members. It is our objective to enhance the lifestyles within our communities and to increase the value of our customer's assets. We will reduce your worries by getting the job done the right way, the first time. We will apply our broad knowledge to bring you cost-effective and timely solutions. You will receive friendly and courteous service. You will be respected and never taken for granted." In the background, a large picture of an eagle holding an American Flag flies over the Blue Ridge Mountains.

In Basslok's farmlands, residence homeowners pay hundreds of dollars but the roads are not repaired, poor landscaping and shrubs go months without trimming and resident managers never call back about complaints. SAC makes accusations of violations based on assumptions of property lines and refuses to provide the name of the person managing the account. There is no ability to provide feedback or complaint

The few "good old southern boys" who run the Board with an iron fist. New Northern-based homeowners who want to clean up the nepotism are restricted by elections held every 24 months. Each period is held by secret ballots and the same members are elected and paid hundreds of dollars per year. It is the American Way under crumbling business establishments managed by modern-day pirates. There is no recourse! In 2023 the HOAs motto is shut up and hand over your monies.

Jack, after many months of tolerating his neighbor, Jubal Johnson, violated HOA rules with encouragement from their management and immunity, had to act. After two community managers state that Jubal has a right to do what he wishes to do on his property, they take his dues and do nothing to stop Jubal Johnson's construction and noise. Finally, after HOA's Mr. Stooley ignores the picture and recording of the construction noise, Jack Von Dimon, requests a face-to-face news interview with Mr. John

Rock, CEO of SAC limited liability, to explain his organization and his continued growth based on the homeowner forced to fund him and his managers.

John Rock refuses and never contacts Jack Von Dimon but refers him to Stooley and Gabe Preston. When homeowners move into an area controlled by the HOA charter, they have no option but to pay over $2,000 for no benefits except for some flowers, trees, and a plastic playground for the children. There is no Community Room or Swimming pool. The money flows into the check accounts of the few executives. Indeed, it is a scam that homeowners should vote and remove the lien on their incomes for no value.

Hidden Neighbors

Near Basslok Plantation stood a three-story, five-bedroom Victorian home with a long driveway that led to the home of a Deputy Sheriff, John Howard, a 42yr old father of two. The Howards' ancestors fought in the Confederacy battles in Virginia and North Carolina. Behind the 100-acre farm property stood two tombstones with the names of Major CSA Phillip Howard (1795 – 1865) and Master Cannon Sergeant, CSA Rusty Howard (1832-1863). Both tombstones have confederate flags that blew in the brisk winds of the winter. The Howards arrived in the South on a convict prison ship from England in 1716. They were sold as indentured servants and worked on the vast Basslok cotton plantations. If they joined the Confederate States of America armed forces they were offered a commission and pay.

The town of Salem was originally designed as a Moravian settlement by Frederick William von Marschall in 1772 as part of the Wachovia Tract. The Moravians had previously bought this 99,000-acre plot of land from Lord Granville in 1753. At first, von Marschall sold the plots of land only to Moravians, which led to some conflict. The restrictions were slowly lifted, and by 1856 the Moravian church ended the lease system.

The Moravians (Old Slavic self-designation Moravljane,[1] Slovak: "Moravania," Czech: Moravané) were a West Slavic tribe in the Early Middle Ages. Although it is not known exactly when the Moravian tribe was founded, Czech historian Dušan Třeštík claimed that the tribe was formed between the turn of the 6th century to the 7th century, around the same time as the other Slavic tribes. In the 9th century, Moravians settled mainly around the historic region of Moravia and Western Slovakia, but also in parts of Lower Austria (up to the Danube) and Upper Hungary.

John Howard was born in Salem North Carolina on a ten-acre farm that grew cotton and wheat for horses. His parents were poor sharecroppers and members of the Moravian church. John was the only child of his parents who would drink homemade whiskey in the evenings. His father would slap his mother and his son when he drank. John was home-schooled on the bible and mathematics. As John reached sixteen years of age, he began to experiment with coca leaves and hashish with his thirteen-year-old girlfriend, Molly, who lived on the next farm. They would play the game of hide and seek. If John won, Molly would have to be tied up in the barn and John would penetrate Molly for ten minutes. Later, Molly told her parents and John was restricted from seeing her. John reacted by being psychologically dependent and becoming an obsessive behavior whose objective is the attainment of pleasure he experienced. John from sixteen years of age began drinking and taking morphine and cocaine. When John's mother died from a heart attack and his father lost the farm, At eighteen, after giving up alcohol and his drugs after AAA, John joined the US Army and fought in the Vietnam War.

At twenty-three, John was discharged and spent three years living on his uncle's farm. At that point, John gave up his alcohol dependence and instead he had fantasies of experiencing the pleasure he had with Molly.

In 2014, John Howard was known in Wake Country as a peace officer who helped many young girls to overcome drug addictions and was given funds to study at North Carolina State University. In 2016, John's wife of ten years disappeared one summer night. The police released her picture as a missing person. John believed she found another man and left to join him in Milwaukee.

In 2015, a fourteen-year-old left her home in Varina to buy some sugar. She never returned home but later her body was found in a sexual position against a tree in the woods. John Howard, on his days off, would stalk, abduct, and rape girls he seduced with money. He wanted to possess the girls he raped. Just seeing them take off their blouse, he would get aroused and then he could not stop until they were strangled with a rope.

In 2017, he abducted two girls, sixteen and seventeen, who were hitchhiking along Highway 70. Once they entered his Jeep Van, they told John that they were running away from their homes as their fathers beat them if they did not complete their homework. They drove for one hour and then John pulled over to a side road and stopped the vehicle saying he had to relieve himself. Then, without another word, he pulled out his service revolver and forced the girls out into the woods. He tied their hands and feet with plastic ties. Then he forced each one to have sex with him. After two hours, he brought them back to his Jeep, blindfolded both, and drove back to his home. Once inside, he untied them and allowed them to have a Pepsi and McDonald's hamburgers. Then he brought both to his basement dungeon and chained them to the wall. At 11 pm, he left to go upstairs to his bedroom to sleep, at 8 am, he had a breakfast of eggs and bacon, and coffee. Then he walked outside to his police car and returned to the Police Station in Raleigh. At 5 pm, John returned home and let the girls out for the bathroom and a meal of fried fish and grits. John said with his gun out, "You both will be safe and I will not harm you, as long you do as I tell you. We are going to be family and in our family, you are my sex slaves." John would take the girls down to the dungeon, beat them up, and then have sexual encounters with them. When he was satisfied, he chained them up and return to his master bedroom to sleep. This routine continues for two months. His dispatcher had notified John while he was on duty that two teenage girls were missing and to be on the lookout for them. Knowing that he could not keep them without drawing suspension, he woke them up on the evening of August 15, 2017. He brought them to the back of his home and told them to run and if they told anyone what happened he would kill them and their parents. The two teenagers were never heard from again in North Carolina.

In 2019, until one of his teenage victims was brought to his home to be sodomized, raped, and forced into a special sex slave hidden room escape, would the local farmers and police learn of the identity of the murderer. John Howard was arrested when he was told to have a meeting with the Sheriff of Wake County. When the office door was open, he was met by two detectives of the North Carolina State Patrol and charged with murder and rape. During his criminal court, John was found guilty and sentenced to a life term without parole. The three teenagers were united with their parents and graduated from the Law School of Duke University and judges of the Wake County Superior Court.

THE EVIL

"On December 15, 21- at 9 am. Jack Von Dimon heard continuous hammering and drilling noises from the backyard when he investigated, he saw Mr. Johnson on top of a large backyard structure 12 inches next to Jack's property fence line. Jack was alarmed by his doing architectural changes again without the HOA's (SAC) approval. Jack reported these violations to the HOA on three separate occasions.

Jubal Johnson said, "I am doing Xmas Decorations." That was not true. When Jack contacted the HOA property Manager, Mr. Stooley, said, "I called Mr. Johnson and confirmed that he was doing Xmas decorations.

Jack was surprised to find Six-foot HOA Basslok's President Gabe Preston at Jack's front door. Jack explained to Gabe what the situation was. Gabe asked his neighbor to go and take some pictures and send them to Mr. Rock and Mr. Stooley. So I took my Canon 35mm and went outside with my camera, with the hope of resolving the situation, Mr. Johnson sat on top of the building's roof and called 911 on his mobile phone angrily staring and me giving me the finger."

Jack thought, gosh, he is recording my conversations. Jack spoke to Jubal, "I wished that we could be friends, and Jubal please get HOA's approval before building all the backyard structures that you've been continually building for the last two years."

To the best of Jack's recollection, "I commented that we should "END" the confrontations and that he follows the HOA rules." Instead, Jubal said, "Jack you would sell your home and move out soon and my family would remain here forever."

Jack spoke, "Listen Jubal, I will not be forced to move because of you or anyone, this is my home." Jack was alarmed by Mr. Johnson for it was clear he was orchestrating a dire event that was in his imagination.

Ten minutes later on 12-15-22, heavily armed County Officers arrived at Jack Von Dimon's estate home. When Jack viewed his security cameras, he believed that he was the one who was claimant and concluded that he could obtain a Restraining Order against Jubal Johnson. Jack could see clearly that there was no criminal matter and just a civil matter with an unbalanced neighbor.

Jack explained to the black Sheriff's Deputy, who had a second armed Deputy standing behind him, what happened as clearly and honestly as he could. They left and walked five minutes to Mr. Johnson's front door. Jubal responded, "Yes, it was a criminal matter. He stated that he would harm me and my family. This is criminal and not a civil matter!" The Deputies returned and said, You must stop contacting or responding to Mr. Johnson." On Christmas Eve of 12-24-22, while installing Christmas lights, Jack fell from the ladder causing two broken ribs and a concussion. Jack lay on the concrete driveway and shouted for help. Gabe and Jubal ignored his screams for help. Jack crawled back into the home and called Wake County EMS. After 30 minutes they arrived and he was placed into the unit and rushed to the hospital. He stayed in the hospital for two days. When he arrived the garage door was still open with the ladder in clear sight.

In extreme pain, on December 29, 2021, Jack Von Dimon took a taxi to RDU to meet his fiancée in Moscow. One week later, they were married in a civil and religious ceremony. Jack said nothing about the events that had him labeled as a criminal according to North Carolina legislative law. On February 16, 2022, at 9 am, Jack returned to Raleigh for the Court date. Jack, could not sleep on the nine-hour flight or at home, "dreaming that he and his new wife would never see each other again. Jack would lose his home and be placed in jail"

Wake County Political Magistrate

After the Civil War ended, the Northern Federal Courts had a goal that former slaves should become judges to demonstrate judicial equity. North Carolina was targeted for its need for judicial reform with a lower court for poor white and black cotton and tobacco sharecroppers. The magistrate was set up and monitored by the former Confederacy lawyers of privilege. A magistrate was to be an independent unbiased judicial officer, recognized by the North Carolina Constitution as an officer of the district court. Magistrates would take the same oath as judges and are subject to the Code of Judicial Conduct. N.C. Const., Art. IV, §10; N.C.G.S. §§7A-170 and 7A-143. The magistrate system received 9% of the NC general fund. Magistrates also provide timely and cost-effective resolutions to civil actions up to $10,000 including summary ejectment (eviction) cases for residential and non-residential properties. Of many civil cases given to the 672 full-time paid Magistrates, one that stands out was to "Hear complaints for temporary Domestic Violence Protective Orders (GS 50B), or temporary Civil No-Contact Orders (50C), where authorized by their local jurisdictions…" This allows for anyone without evidence except by swearing that any minor issue can be accelerated into a criminal matter to be heard by the Superior court.

Magistrate Crystal Lina grew up in a two-bedroom shack with her nine siblings. Her grandparents worked in the cotton fields from 7 am to 7 pm each day with time off on Sundays for Baptist Church Services. At 3 pm they returned to work on the 300 acres of the sixth Basslok Family farming area. Like many black children, she grew up believing that they were victims of the "Southern White oppressors." Crystal also had a dream to attend college and become a judge to punish whites who brought so much pain to her ancestors. Crystal attended a private Baptist black university in Raleigh, North Carolina. After graduating, Crystal became a paralegal and attended a diverse University in Virginia obtaining an MA in Criminal Justice and Corrections. In the evenings, to prepare for the LSAT and the NC bar, she took online University correspondence courses for diverse students in Law. Standards for black lawyers for the NC Bar were lowered. Crystal Lina's Affirmative Action credentials led to a Deputy Clerk salaried position in Raleigh for five years and when NC had its first Democratic Governor and North Carolina received massive immigration from Democratic-controlled Northern cities, she became a local Black Female Magistrate in February 2021.

In December 2021, Jubal Johnson filed his criminal complaint before Magistrate Crystal Lina, who without witnesses or proof, ordered that Jack Von Dimon face a criminal judicial hearing in the Raleigh Superior Court.

Wake County Meritorious Judges

"Established in 1777, the superior courts are North Carolina's oldest courts. Superior courts hear civil and criminal cases. The superior court is divided into five divisions and 48 districts across the state. Every six months, superior court judges rotate among the districts within their divisions. The rotation system is provided for by the state constitution and is designed to minimize conflicts of interest that might result from having a permanent judge in one district. Each administrative superior court district has a senior resident superior court judge who manages the administrative duties of the court. A clerk of the superior court is elected in each county and is responsible for all clerical and record-keeping functions."

Superior court judges are elected by the voters in their district, must reside in the district in which they are elected, and serve terms of eight years.

According to the North Carolina state constitution, "all judges must be attorneys. However, they are prohibited from practicing law privately while they are judges. They also must be under the age of 72, the mandatory retirement age for judges. When a vacancy occurs in a regular judgeship (usually through death or retirement), or a new judgeship is created by the General Assembly, the governor fills the vacancy by appointing a judge to fill the position until the next general election or for the remainder of the former judge's term in office."

In 2020, the lawyer Raymond Cooper, the Democratic Governor of NC, appointed Democratic Party member Mark Stevens to serve as District Court Judge in Judicial District 10C for Wake County, filling the seat of the Honorable Robert Rader. Stevens graduated with a BA from Denison University earning his Juris Doctorate from North Carolina Central University. The Raleigh native served as an Assistant District Attorney in Wake County since 2008 and held leadership roles with the Wake County Bar Association.

After 26 years on the bench, Chief District Court Judge Robert B. Rader, a 1985 graduate of Campbell Law School, has announced his retirement from the bench effective Monday, Aug. 31, 2020. Unlike, attorney Mark Stevens, Judge Rader had a strong commitment to the South's historic preservation is perhaps best demonstrated by his involvement in the Yates Mill Associates, Inc., a private non-profit corporation that preserved Wake County's last surviving grist mill (circa 1756) and established Historic Yates Mill County Park. Judge Rader was involved in the planning of the new Court House, a 577,000 sq. ft. state-of-the-art building months ahead of schedule and 30 million dollars below budget.

Rader grew up in Morganton, where he and Justice Sam Ervin IV were high school classmates and where Judge Sam Ervin III of the Fourth U.S. Circuit Court of Appeals was a regular in his father's restaurant. Sam Evin was a folk hero who was Chairman of the Watergate Hearings. "Samuel James Ervin Jr. was an American politician. A Democrat, he served as a U.S. Senator from North Carolina from 1954 to 1974. A native of Morganton, he liked to call himself a "country lawyer", and often told humorous stories in his Southern drawl."

Masterful Attorney of the Law

Due to a criminal misdemeanor court action of December 2021, taken on the part of Jack Von Dimon's next-door neighbor, Jack was clear that his new neighbor's false statements required that he retain a legal advocate. Considering Jubal Johnson's behavior when Jack first moved to North Carolina from California, Jack knew that he needed to locate an attorney who had a great criminal law reputation in the County Court System. Jack had interviewed four other lawyers who solicited him by mail that they would consider the case, prepare, and provide a great defense. Over five months of collaborating with Attorney Asim, I found him to be a fearless lawyer focused on the pursuit of justice.

Stephen Asim was a Former Prosecutor with Experience in Over 100,000 County Criminal Cases & Trials. Attorney Asim spent the bulk of his career as a County District Attorney and is known as an effective criminal lawyer. He has tried over 2,000 trials with charges ranging from simple assault to first-degree murder. Asim Law experienced over 60,000 Wake County criminal charges. In his time as a district attorney, Attorney Asim held positions as the military liaison of the District Attorney's Office, and a member of the felony drug unit. He spent over a year as a member of and as the legal advisor for Wake County's stop drunk driving Task Force.

North Carolina law categorizes criminal offenses into two separate categories: misdemeanors and felonies. "The criminal code is massive, and the type and severity of crimes covered under each category can vary greatly. Misdemeanors are considered less serious than felonies but can still carry possible jail time, and huge fines, and will permanently appear on a criminal background check. Felony charges are categorized into ten different classes based on severity, with a Class A Felony considered the most serious and a Class One felony the least serious. The North Carolina felony punishment chart can be found below. Being convicted of a felony will undoubtedly affect you for the rest of your life. This status affects your right to vote, own firearms, travel, and acquire certain state-issued licenses. Felons will also face huge obstacles in finding employment and renting residential and commercial property.

When Jack Von Dimon walked into Asim's seventh-story office overlooking the city of Raleigh, he knew that great chemistry existed between the two men. After a brief cup of tea, Jack turned to Stephen and commented, "! Wonder how a man of my credentials finds himself being bullied by a high school grad from North Carolina and with a rap sheet of 7 arrests. It is obvious that these "rednecks" enjoys making up platters of pain when they live next door to a man who served and wounded in Vietnam- who worked his way to his MBA must face NC's legion of haters like the HOA run by CEO Rock who give preferences to buy a homeowner who has no Funds but young children but beware of those who buy homes in the South that were raised in the NORTH. I know that game." Stephen let out a smile, "Jack remember when you move into an HOA real-estate area, you assume new owners are screened but they are not. They just want your money. It is as if each of the 100 homes in your development is an ATM that they collect to build up a semi-bank to steal your money and do nothing but pay the four or five dopes on the HOA committee or I should say, the good old boys." They both laughed and moved on to discuss the case and strategy if it goes to actual court. Jack moved in his chair and pull some notes from his briefcase. "Stephen you can see Jubal made a Magistrate complaint on December 15, 2021, just ten days before Christmas, writing "that I have communicated threats; namely, I will 'end' you and you will not live forever. Of course, that was preposterous as I was meaning that our arguments should end and let us be friends. We can live forever waiting." Stephen let me show you the pictures I took that day. I sent them to Mr. Preston, Rock, and the Community Manager." When the officer arrived at my door the first time, he concluded after talking to Jubal that this was not a criminal manner but civil. Stephen was relaxed and confident. "Don't worry we will change the court date and prepare our strategies. We will meet on the second floor before the proceedings." With that, both men shook hands and talked for five minutes about Jack's marriage in Eastern Europe in January and returning in February.

On December 29, 2021, Jack flew on Aeroflot from RDU and directly to Moscow. Since Jack had full CCTV cameras on the property, he saw and heard a female Deputy Sheriff at his door for five days from the 24th of December to the first week of January 2022. Jack's security call center recorded her saying, "I know you in there. Open this door now! Your neighbors Preston and Johnson said you are in the home hiding." As Jack and his wife relaxed at the five-star Renaissance Hotel six thousand miles away, they both smiled and kissed. Even with Jack's broken ribs and the concussion he suffered, they were happy together.

What is legally considered a "threat" in North Carolina?

Section 14-277.1 - Communicating threats

(a) A person is guilty of a Class 1 misdemeanor if without lawful authority:

(1) He willfully threatens to physically injure the person or that person's child, sibling, spouse, or dependent or willfully threatens to damage the property of another;

(2) The threat is communicated to the other person, orally, in writing, or by any other means;

(3) The threat is made in a manner and under circumstances that would cause a reasonable person to believe that the threat is likely to be carried out; and

(4) The person threatened believes that the threat will be carried out.

Criminal Court Prep Time

*Was there pre-mediation of the alleged crime?

*Was there intent? Is this circumstantial?

*Where are the witnesses? Beyond a reasonable doubt?

*Who is the plaintiff's Attorney? Does she have a background as a prosecutor?

*Be well prepared... How should I look?

*Can you give me some questions that might be asked of me?

*Stress who I am? = I have high character and career accomplishments.

Courtesy of the Wake County Superior Court, Raleigh NC.

The North Carolina District Courts utilize partisan elections in the selection of judges. District judges serve four-year terms, after which they must run for re-election if they wish to continue serving. From March 23, 2017, the North Carolina legislature changed the method of election to partisan elections by overriding Gov. Roy Cooper's veto of HB 100. This change was effective in the 2018 district court. The district court hears criminal cases involving misdemeanors and infractions (non-jury).

Wake County 9 am - Superior Court Pre-trial Examination

On February 18, 2022, Jack arrived at the 9 am ordered filing by the Superior Court in Court Room Nine. Jack watched as all defendants who were Black were given special attention by the presiding judge. Without lunch, at 1400 hours, Jack agreed to Mediation and paid the 150 dollars fee. Three hours later, He met Jubal with a Black Court Mediator in a small room outside the Court. Jubal would not give any eye contact and stare at the Mediator only. Jack said, "I would like to live in peace with Jubal and be his friend." Jubal grew angry and screamed at the Mediator, "I do not want mediation. I want this criminal case to be heard by the judge. He tried to kill me and my family." Jack said nothing as the mediator tried to resolve the issues between the two. Jubal just demanded my jailing and that I was a danger to him as I said I was going to "end his life and his family." Jack took a deep breath and knew that now he had to face the Court. Also, he realized that he could never be a neighbor to his liking if I objected to his violations of Neighborhood peace and tranquility. The mediator said, "Jubal does not want to resolve the issue. This is over. The best to both of you."

Before he became a judge, Dan Nagle served in the Wake County Sheriff's Office for 28 years. After he retired, Nagle earned his J.D. and then interned with the North Carolina Supreme Court. He then worked for the Wake County District Attorney's Office, the Wake County Public Defender's Office, and the law firm of Hatch, Little, and Bunn, LLP. Immediately before his election to the bench, Nagle worked as an assistant district attorney with the District Attorney's Office for the 10th Judicial District.

When Jack Von Dimon entered the Court, the biased and political Judge Nagle was leaving for the day. The criminal proceedings were rescheduled as Attorney Asim was still present to represent Jack. Attorney Asim had been in Court for two days waiting as Jack did. Jack thanked him and the case was rescheduled for a Judge known as a man of integrity and justice.

Criminal Trial by a Judicial Officer

On April 8, 2022, at Wake County at 9 am, proceeding before the honorable Judge Stevens, Asim's skill in the cross-examination phase became very apparent. He demonstrated the truth of the case to the Court and Jack's innocence. I am honored to consider him a good friend and a knowledgeable attorney. Steven believed in the Constitution and the defense of my right to "life, liberty, and the pursuit of happiness."

Two weeks later, after Jack's marriage in Europe, Jack sat in a vacant courtroom, except for the Presiding Judge, Jubal's attorneys, and Jack Von Dimon's attorney. Asim asked to address the court. The attorneys, plaintiff, and defendant moved into the hearing arena. Jubal was called first and presented his case. His female attorney questioned him, and Attorney Asim also asked questions. Next, Jack who was a Disabled Combat

Vietnam Veteran who had his ankles, toes, and hips surgically removed and replaced with metal implants, slowly entered the docket and took his oath, to tell the truth. Jack sat and saw Jubal staring at him with intense anger.

Jack spoke, "Jack Von Dimon walked to the docket, took the oath administered by the Superior Court Judge, and spoke with power and clarity, "For 30yrs, I had a great technology career In California's Silicon Valley. In addition, I was a University Professor for 13yrs and moved to NC, to continue my writing and publishing career. My dream was a home in a good neighborhood of loving people and peaceful surroundings. I am a 100% disabled decorated Combat Veteran of the Vietnam War. Today, I have complete removal and replacement of both ankles, toes, and hips. Also, I am a father of three and two grandchildren. I am not guilty of this allegation that I would harm anyone especially Mr. Jubal Johnson who I tried from my move to the Black Forest HOA from California to be his friend and neighbor. I placed a postcard from my novel, Angels in the Silicon, to say hello. Mr. Johnson took Umbridge and within a few months expressed that I should go back to Silicon Valley and not live in NC. I have a lot of love and respect for those who show me the same. I believe I am good and fair to all neighbors. Mr. Johnson was not following the HOA architectural rules and I told him so after Gabe and his neighbors told me of their mutual concerns. I sent emails to Mr. Rock and Mr. Stooley about the noise and the building of this structure next to my property. Mr. Johnson said that he was only building Christmas decorations that were false. I was then asked to take pictures and send them to Mr. Stooley. Later, I sent them to Mr. Rock as well. When I did, Mr. Johnson was on top of the roof about 23 feet off the ground and peering down. Jubal became agitated and said he was calling 911 because I was abusing him. I said let's be friends. Then he stated to the best of my recollection that "he would live here forever and that I would not live here forever, and I would move soon" Judge, I said, that no one can live here forever. I will end this confrontation and I am not moving."

After two hours of skillful Legal questioning of Jack and Jubal, the Judge made his ruling. "I have reviewed the facts of this criminal case. Jack Von Dimon is not guilty of the misdemeanor charge of communicating threats, and my ruling is not subject to appeal. "

Jack stood up and hugged Asim. Jubal's body sank into his chair and stared at Judge Steven with anger. Jubal was unhappy. The judge said, "Mr. Jubal Johnson will now leave the Court Room and the Court Building. Mr.Jack Von Dimon will wait 20 minutes before leaving in case there might be a confrontation between the parties. I want to thank the attorneys and their clients. Thank you."

Jack was relieved of the stress and burden placed on him by the lies of Jubal. Jack shook Attorney Asim's hand and thanked him. Jack left the Court Room with a renewed respect for the justice that was rendered. He took the elevator to the first floor, walked to the front door where five sheriff deputies were standing nearby, and walked into the wind of a typical Raleigh late afternoon.

Justice – a Double Edge Sword of Faith

Several months later, on April 3, 2022, Jack Von Dimon was planting some flowers near the back of his residential property. Jubal Johnson started to make sounds near the fence and continued pounding with his hammer for over two hours. He got some type of angry response as he did in December 2021. Jack did nothing. Jack believed in forgiveness and "love thy neighbor as yourself". Jack tried to be Jubal's friend and Jack decided to use a recorder and asked, over the fence, to be Jubal Johnson's friend. Jubal, screamed over the fence, " I will never be your friend, you must move!."

In May 2022, a For Sale sign stood in front of Jubal's home.

Jubal's placed his home for sale against the wishes of his wife Mary Beth. In June 2022, Mary Beth moved out of the home and took her boys as well, She filed for divorce over the 24 months of Jubal's fixation with the harassment of his neighbors and especially Jack Von Dimon. Even after selling for over $650,000 and buying a new home, Mary Beth refused to move in with Jubal.

This was a bad movie over nothing but within the reflecting mind of Jubal Johnson. Instead of negotiating, following the HOA rules, and being a good neighbor, Jubal drank and decided to fight his neighbors. The result was he lost his family and his home. Jubal did not respect his elders and believed he was fighting against a "Northerner Yankee" who robbed his ancestors of their lands.

CLOSING

"When we see in others the same spirit that lives in us, we feel as if we have awakened from a long sleep." Leo Tolstoy 1885

Courtesy of the Wake County Board of Commissioners (Shinica Thomas as chair and Susan Evans as vice chair of the board for 2023. Don Mial and Cheryl Stallings, and incumbent commissioners, Vickie Adamson and Matt Calabria].

Safe Neighborhoods

Never enter the Court without a good lawyer who believes in Justice. Jack Von Dimon was fortunate to have found an attorney who was unique and strove for justice. Jack had spent years in California's Silicon Valley in Technology Management and as a University Professor. Currently, he lives in Charlotte North Carolina, and runs his own business in Publishing and Aerospace Research. Jack Von Dimon called up Haldor after his criminal case was settled in his favor, "I had experience in technology and management fields for over twenty-plus years that gave me a clear insight into professionals who are honest and dedicated to their career of choice. Anyone who retains Steven Asim's representation will be working with a Law Firm that preserves justice. He is a true American Constitution scholar. Just remember Haldor, never enter the Court without a good lawyer who believes in Justice. " Haldor replied, "Jack before your court date, Jubal came over to my home and demanded that I go to the Court and be his witness as to your lack of character and threatening actions. Well, I set him straight. I told Jubal that I was your friend and I strongly objected to Jubal demanding that I stand up for his criminal accusations that you Jack, planned to kill his family. I told him to get the hell off of my lawn and get lost!"

Friends are far between in moving into a new neighborhood, but Haldor demonstrated what love and truth are all about.

Domestic Abuse

According to the National Statistics Domestic Violence Fact Sheet, "On average, nearly 20 people per minute are physically abused by an intimate partner in the United States. During one year, this equates to more than 10 million women and men. 19.3 million women and 5.1 million men in the United States have been stalked in their lifetime.60.8% of female stalking victims and 43.5% of men reported being stalked by a current or former intimate partner. A study of intimate partner homicides found that 20% of victims were not the intimate partners themselves, but family members, friends, neighbors, persons who intervened, law enforcement responders, or bystanders. Physical, mental, and sexual and reproductive health effects have been linked with intimate partner violence including adolescent pregnancy, unintended pregnancy in general, miscarriage, stillbirth, intrauterine hemorrhage, nutritional deficiency, abdominal pain and other gastrointestinal problems, neurological disorders, chronic pain, disability, anxiety and post-traumatic stress disorder (PTSD), as well as non-communicable diseases such as hypertension, cancer, and cardiovascular diseases. Victims of domestic violence are also at higher risk for developing addictions to alcohol, tobacco, or drugs."

Listed on safealliance.org, "one in four women will experience domestic violence during her lifetime. Three women are killed every day in America by their intimate partners and more than 15 million children are exposed to domestic violence every year... The numbers demonstrate that incidents of domestic violence are not as far removed as one may think. Domestic violence can impact anyone, regardless of gender, race, age, sexual orientation, religion, socioeconomic background, or education."

Mean-Spirited Neighbors

Jubal Johnson got on the stand and weaved his story that Jack Von Dimon was going "to kill him and possibly his family." What a stretch that was! Jack allowed his very competent attorney, Stephen Asim, to mount a great defense. Jack did go on the stand. In the end. Jubal lost what mattered most. To put it simply, the Judge declared Jack Von Dimon not guilty. Unfortunately, Jubal will never be a trusting neighbor and Jack will not recognize or speak to neighbors who act unhinged. Jack can only pray for Jubal as he has some major mental issues, but then Jack did not want to judge Jubal but pray for him. So, it all went well. Jack's case was expunged by his superior attorney next Monday. Jack felt good. Jack learned a lot about human nature; namely, to be careful when you reach out in a friendly manner to neighbors who have not proven their worth.

Jack celebrated his good fortune with his new wife and his large family.

Jubal would buy a new Hillsborough home but he lost his family. During a major thunderstorm, lightning strikes Jubal's Hillsborough and burns down the two-story $650.000 home. Mary Beth gains a new management position at Bank of American in Charlotte North Carolina. Jubal is given supervision visitation rights on Saturdays and Sundays. Jubal is ordered by the Court to pay spousal and child support of $4,390.87 per month. Shortly after, It was heard that Jubal left for Ukraine and joined the Azov Battalion in Kharkiv.

Bibliography

Anderson John, "A Warrior's Wisdom and Weaknesses." Life and Arts, The Wall Street Journal, Page A13, Friday, May 22, 2020

Animated Civil War Map, The Civil War Animated Battle Map: April 12, 1861 – May 9, 1865

Basslok, Malinda Sarah, "Woman of War: Sarah Malinda Basslok," (2011), from North Carolina Civil War Trails, in the North Carolina Digital Collections, https://digital.ncdcr.gov/digital/collection/p15012coll8/id/10777/

Ellis, Ted (2017). Braddock's Neglected Route The Lost Fork of the COnococheague Road. Columbia, SC, USA. ISBN 9780998833002.

Flannery, Christopher, "American Christmas, American New Year"-Imprimis. 12 2022 Volume 51, Number 12. P.12.

Gordon John Steele, The Epic History of American Economic Power. Imprimis, January 2922, Volume 51, Number 1, "Inflation in the U.S".

Heulon Dean Photo Collection, PhC.133, North Carolina State Archives, call #: PhC133_1957_293. Available from https://www.flickr.com/photos/north-carolina-state-archives/5716977046/ (accessed June 27, 2012).

History of Germany: Youtube: https://www.dukeupress.edu/german-women-for-empire-1884-1945

Jason L. Riley, Senior fellow Manhattan Institute and Wall Street Journal columnist. Imprimis, March 2022, Volume 51, Number 3 "The Continuing Importance of Thomas Sowell."

John Anderson, "A Warrior's Wisdom and Weaknesses." Life and Arts, The Wall Street Journal, Page A13, Friday, May 22, 2020

John Steele Gordon, The Epic History of American Economic Power. Imprimis, January 2922, Volume 51, Number 1, "Inflation in the U.S".

Library of Congress. Civil War Still Photographs.. https://www.youtube.com/watch?v=4Y56oMBcklo

Mary Meet, Murder - Season 1, Episode 34 - Parsons - Full Episode, FilmRise True Crime

Morrisville NC Historical Society, https://www.ncpedia.org/gsearch?query=BASSLOK

North Carolina Rules for Magistrates https://www.nccourts.gov/documents/publications/north-carolina-rules-of-conduct-for-magistrates

North Carolina Rules: https://www.nccourts.gov/assets/documents/publications/NCMagistrates_FactSheet_2020-21_WEB_FINAL_1.pdf?

Owens Candace, "Blackout" Threshold Editions, Simon & Schuster Inc., NY. 2020.

Richard Jerome, The Civil War, Life Explores, Meredeth Corporation, NewYork, NY. 2020

Riley Jason L., Senior fellow Manhattan Institute and Wall Street Journal columnist. Imprimis, March 2022, Volume 51, Number 3 "The Continuing Importance of Thomas Sowell."

Simms Brendan, "Europe -The Struggle for Supremacy, from 1453 to the Present, Basic Books-Perseus Books, NY, 2014.

Tobacco- Part 1: Introduction; Tobacco- Part 2: Development and Growth of the North Carolina Tobacco Industry. Tobacco- Part 3: The Rise of "Big Tobacco"; Tobacco- Part 4: Legal Challenges and the Decline of the Industry; Tobacco- Part 5: References)

Vervais Mindy, North Carolina Lawyers Weekly on October 27, 2020. Her article, "Domestic Violence Awareness Month"

End Notes

What to do or not to do with New Neighbors?

[Contributed by courtesy of Forbes: https://www.forbes.com/sites/trulia/2015/01/25/end-these-6-bad-neighbor-behaviors/?sh=ed75d3b212bb]

"A neighbor from hell is someone who lacks empathy toward those living near." These are people who enjoy conflict, which makes them particularly hard to topple. (And why many good neighbors often move away.)-

1. Noisy: Making noise is the number-one complaint people have about their neighbors. Whether it's loud music, barking dogs, or out-of-control parties, noise, especially during sleeping hours, can get under people's skin. (What NOT to do: Don't bang on walls or ceilings or try to fight fire with fire by turning up your music to drown out theirs.)

2. Harasser: Though most neighbor complaints begin with a noise issue, they can end up in the realm of harassment. "More people are reflexively choosing to be aggressive toward anyone complaining, rather than working things out," says Borzotta. (What NOT to do: Do not react in anger. Stay on the right. Never resort to tit-for-tat behaviors.)

3. Home-value crasher: This neighbor has a house in disrepair, an overgrown lawn, or junk in his front yard. Neighbors hate this guy because he brings down the resale value of their homes — and people get serious when you mess with their wallets. (What NOT to do: Don't offer to "fix" his yard. Nothing will incense a person faster than your presumption.)

4. Criminal: Violence, vandalism, peeping, and petty theft: — these are among the issues you could be facing in the form of domestic disputes, threats, stealing of yard tools, and the presence of sex offenders in your neighborhood. All of which can present a very real danger. (What TO do: If you suspect there is an issue, tell others in your community. Neighborhood vigilance deters criminal activity. Notify the proper authorities if you witness any truly criminal behaviors.)

5. Simple guidelines

6. Communicate: Get to know your neighbors. Open, direct, and polite communication is key.

7. Escalate slowly: If polite communication has failed to provide results, don't turn your dial immediately to 911. Instead, think of the next minimal step you can take toward resolution. Can you talk over coffee? Is there a manager, landlord, or homeowner association that can intervene on your behalf?

Are there other organizations that can provide support, such as neighborhood associations, animal control, sanitation, the city, or the police? If all else fails, seek the advice of an expert like Borzotta or the counsel of a professional mediator or lawyer.

8. Always document: (As soon as an issue starts, begin taking notes with dates, times, photos, and any potential updates or retaliation. This will come in handy should you need to seek outside help.)

Final

(The characters and events portrayed, and the names herein are fictitious. And any similarity to the name and character or history of any person is coincidental and unintentional. Any actual persons and events in this story are included for realism. And are entirely unrelated to the fictional characters and events.)

END "Wake County — 9 am©®" by Richard Theodor Kusiolek

Printed in the United States
by Baker & Taylor Publisher Services